# PUPPY PRIMER

BRENDA SCIDMORE &
PATRICIA B. MCCONNELL, PH.D.

For information, contact:
Dog's Best Friend, Ltd.
P.O. Box 447
Black Earth, WI 53515
608/767-2435
www.dogsbestfriendtraining.com

Printed in the United States of America

# CONTENTS

Introduction .................................................................*i*

**Chapter 1: Socialization** ..............................................1
  *Socialization*                                    *1*
  *Teaching Come*                                    *4*
  *Teaching Sit*                                     *8*
  *Teaching Down*                                    *9*

**Chapter 2: Play–Biting & Housetraining** ..........................11
  Puppy Biting                                       11
  Housetraining                                      14
  Sit and Down Revisited                             19
  Come                                               21
  Teaching Stand                                     23
  Socialization                                      24

**Chapter 3: Verbal Praise & Corrections** ...................... 25
  Verbal Praise                                      25
  Corrections                                        26
  Sit–Down–Stand                                     30
  Come                                               31
  Walking By Your Side                               32
  "Belly Up," or "Play Dead"                         35

**Chapter 4: Play** .......................................... 37
  Play While Training                                37
  When Play Backfires                                43
  Stealing                                           45

**Chapter 5: Raising Confident Puppies**..........................................  **47**

    Fear in Puppies                    47

    Children & Puppies             49

    Puppy Stay           50

    Jumping Up          51

    Crate Training         52

**Chapter 6: Adolescence & Other Quandaries** ..........................  **55**

    Ignoring Commands         55

    Dog to Dog Interactions      56

    Submissive Urination       57

    Multiple Dog Households    58

    Puppies Home Alone       59

    Car Sickness          60

    Exercise             60

    Barking               61

    What's Next?          63

# INTRODUCTION

Good Puppy Owner! Goooood Puppy Owner! How clever of you to start now on your puppy's education! You should feel good that you are caring and committed enough to take responsibility for your warm, furry little creature's total welfare. There's more to your puppy's well-being than just her physical health, as you well know! How your dog interacts as an adult, with you and the rest of her world, is determined to a large extent by the environment you provide for her now. Acquainting her with the intricacies of human and canine society will help shape her ultimate temperament and character during this oh-so-important phase of puppy-hood.

The days of letting your pup grow up under the front porch chasing the mailman and roaming the neighborhood are over. Perhaps that lifestyle provided more exercise, and a thrill of adventure, but it certainly provided hazards as well. Today, with a higher density of human habitation, we need to keep our dogs closer to us and to have more control over their actions. Our dogs need training, supervision, joyful exercise, and clear boundaries. We need to actively raise our dogs to be well-mannered citizens.

As we integrate our dogs more directly into our lives, we are expecting more from them. At the same time, we are learning they have much to offer us, and caring own-ers are realizing the importance of building a good working relationship between themselves and their canine companions.

The question of course, is how do we do achieve these things? How do we let our pups know what will be expected of them? How do we build a relationship with another species that will allow us to live harmoniously together for the next 10-15 years? It can be hard enough to communicate effectively with our own species! So how do we go about doing so with our four-legged friends? By endeavoring to learn all we can about them: to understand them *as dogs*, rather than looking at them as furry little humans.

Lassies are made, not born. Your dog doesn't come into this world with the ability to read your mind, or even to understand English. And by the same token, you were not born instinctively knowing how to train a dog. Training a dog involves some knowledge and physical skills (primarily timing) that anyone can learn, if they are willing to invest some time and energy. The man who trained Lassie had to learn those skills just like the rest of us. He wasn't born knowing how to train animals any more than you were. We all start from the same place.

We are delighted that you chose to start your journey with us! Our goal in this book is to teach you what we know about your pup's development, and how your puppy *thinks, communicates,* and *learns.* Involve the whole family, it's an adventure best shared by all. You'll get the most out of this book by reading it one chapter at a time (each chapter conforms to one week of Dog's Best Friend, Ltd. puppy socialization class). Best of all, read this with your pup by your side so you can try things out.

*Think of training your pup as a fun new sport. Like all sports, the more you learn and the more you practice, the better you'll be and the more fun you'll have. Let the games begin!*

# Chapter 1

# SOCIALIZATION

**In this chapter:**
*Socialization..............1*
*Teaching Come ..........4*
*Teaching Sit ..............8*
*Teaching Down ..........9*

Probably the single most important thing you can do to help your puppy grow up to be a friendly, confident, reliable, and happy family member, is to *socialize* your puppy now.

## *What Does Socialization Mean?*

Socialization means giving your pup careful, positive exposure to all of the things that they might encounter as an adult dog. It's vital to do this as soon as possible while your pup is still in the "critical" or "sensitive" period of socialization, which starts with their moms at about 3 weeks of age and continues through approximately 12-14 weeks of age.

Puppies need continued socialization throughout their lives, especially the first year. However, the "critical" or "sensitive" period of determining social relationships comes only once in your dog's life. It is called a "critical" or "sensitive" period because a relatively small amount of change in your puppy's life now, has a tremendous lifelong effect on your dog's future behavior.

Socialization now, during this very impressionable period will help your pup to grow up to be friendly and confident.

## *Why Is Socialization Important?*

If a puppy isn't exposed to a variety of people (including children) and other dogs during this sensitive period, they might never be friendly or confident with people or other dogs when they become adults. Fear in puppies is often exhibited as aggression in adult dogs.

This critical socialization period is the age when puppies are predisposed to accepting:

    1) People of all types, shapes, sizes and ages.
    2) Dogs and all other animals they might encounter as an adult (cats, horses, guinea pigs, etc.).
    3) Changes in their environments.

At 7–8 weeks of age (when most puppies leave the litter and are taken to their new homes), a puppy's brain is still developing. Right now your pup is at the age when she is learning at a faster rate than she ever will be again, at any time in her life. The level of an adult dog's internal complexity will be dependent on the level of environmental complexity she receives between approximately 2 weeks of age, and about 14–16 weeks of age.

Your pup is learning how to learn right now. She can become versatile and adaptable because of her early experiences, or she can become socially, intellectually, and developmentally stunted.

For example, if a pup grows up in an empty room (or on a chain in a yard), without any environmental input, that's about all she will be equipped to deal with as an adult. A dog like this would not know how to interact with adults, children, other dogs, cats, cars, vacuums, televisions, ringing telephones, umbrellas, brooms, or the smell of perfume.

Regardless of whether your pup lives with you quietly alone, or in a large hustling and bustling household, you *must* get your pup out and about to experience the world while your pup is still young. In order to cope with life in human society all puppies need to be exposed *now* to as many situations as possible that she might encounter as an adult. Take full advantage of this golden opportunity to influence (in a very positive way) the development of your dog's eventual temperament and character.

Puppies need to get three primary things out of their socialization experiences:

    1) They need to learn how to play, with other dogs and with people.
    2) They need to learn how to cope with change, whether it's meeting a new dog or moving to a new house.
    3) They need to learn how to sort out conflict now, before they get to an age when conflicts can be more serious.

### When To Socialize Your Pup

**Now!** Do as much socializing as possible in the coming weeks and throughout the entire first year of your pup's life. Ideally, socialization should be ongoing throughout your dog's life. Don't ever stop socializing, but pay special attention to it right now.

## *Where To Socialize Your Pup*

**Everywhere!** Socialize your pup everywhere that you can take her safely and legally. Get her out and about a lot. Teach her to ride in the car, to visit the vet's office or groomer's shop, to be comfortable at the park, in a dog training class, in a hotel room, in a tent, at friends' houses, in a boarding kennel, on grass, on pavement; any place that you might take her as an adult. In general, go to a wide variety of places.

**You should know**, however, that there is *some risk* of disease involved when young puppies are exposed to the world at large before they've been fully vaccinated. Most pups do not get their last set of puppy vaccinations until about 16 weeks of age, but the critical period of socialization is from about 3 weeks to about 12 to 14 weeks of age. If you wait until your pup is fully vaccinated, you risk inadequate socialization; but if you take your pup out and about, you risk disease. It's a compromise either way, and a decision you have to make for yourself. Keep in mind, though, the indications are that many more dogs die from behavioral problems than from disease. Talk to your vet about ways to cut the risks, while still taking advantage of this sensitive, critical period of socialization.

## *With Whom Do You Need To Socialize Your Pup?*

Expose your pup to lots of other people (see special note below about children). Keep in mind that just because you have more than one person in the house doesn't mean your puppy will know how to deal with anyone other than household members. Puppies need to be exposed to many different people in order to generalize the idea that people overall are okay.

Similarly, just because you have children doesn't necessarily mean that your pup will be good with all children. Puppies must be exposed, under careful supervision, to many different children, making sure it's always a positive encounter.

All dogs will encounter children, sometime, somewhere, at some point in their existence even if you don't have children yourself. When that does happen, your dog will most likely be more comfortable, confident and appropriate with them only if he had a chance to be exposed to them during this critical period of his development.

Children look different, sound different, smell different, and especially move differently than adults. Children tend to make more sudden and erratic movements than adults. Pups need to learn that all of these differences between children and adults are nothing to be afraid of.

Don't be fooled into thinking that because you have another dog your puppy will be socialized to other dogs. Your pup needs to meet many other dogs and needs to interact with them in order to learn all the rules of polite canine-to-canine encounters. Your pup should also meet various different types of dogs: big ones, small ones, broad ones, squat ones, ones that snort or breathe loudly, long-legged ones, short, low to the ground ones,…well, you get the idea! Interactions should all be with relatively friendly dogs so your pup has lots of positive experiences and learns to trust other dogs, not to be frightened of them.

## COME

Ironically, the more control we have over our dogs, the more freedom we can give them (and the safer we can keep them). Clearly the "come" command is one of the most important signals you can teach your puppy. It's the command you will be spending the most time practicing.

Ultimately we'd all like a dog that will come reliably anytime we ask, wherever we are, regardless of whatever distractions are present. That's a tall order! But it's a reasonable one for a well trained adult dog. It is asking *too much* of your puppy right now (or for many months), but now is the time to start building the foundation that will accomplish that kind of control in the future.

Right now your puppy is at an age when she's focused on you. However as she becomes an adolescent and then an adult, her attention will be more easily drawn away from you onto the myriad of interesting things out there in the world. Things like squirrels and cats and handsome strutting Labradors will compete for your dog's attention. However, you can take advantage of your young pup's current focus on you by *conditioning* her to love to come when you call! With training and practice it will eventually become an easy habit for her to obey the word "come," even with all those enticing distractions around.

"Conditioning" means to *associate* a stimulus with a specific response. Remember when you were a kid and you heard your parents say something like: "Joe quit that…Joseph quit doing that,…JOSEPH ALAN SMITH stop it right NOW!!" Boy, when that middle name came out, you knew it was serious! No more dawdling for you! Your middle name, used in that context, became your signal (*or conditioned stimulus*) for a change in attitude (your response). You learned to associate that phrase with quick compliance…or else!

Used in a more positive light, we can actively condition our pups to associate the signal "come" with the pleasure of running to us (the response). We can do this in a

4

number of ways, lots of movement on our part being the primary one. Dogs love to chase moving targets. So why not make yourself the center of your puppy's attention by becoming the very best moving target around?! She'll be thrilled! You'll take on a new appeal if she can chase you, especially if you play "hard to get."

Add the word "come" just before she starts to run toward you, and you'll be on your way to a pup that associates the word "come" with "Aha, the game's afoot!!"

## SOME THINGS TO KEEP IN MIND
## WHEN TEACHING YOUR PUPPY "COME"

### Signals

- Animals learn best when they initiate an action on their own. Reeling your pup in on a leash is forcing him to approach. It's much more effective to get him to approach you voluntarily, and then put that action on cue by calling him *just before he initiates* his approach toward you.

- Decide as a family what word you will use to call your dog. Choose a word or phrase and make sure everyone in the family uses that and only that, so as not to confuse your puppy.

- How you use your voice is an important factor. A good signal to use is your dog's name, said in a relatively flat tone, followed by the word "come!" said in a rising, higher tone.

- Clapping is one of the most effective noises we know of to motivate your dog to come to you. Hand-claps, whistles, or high pitched, rapidly repeated notes like "pup pup pup pup!" are good acoustic signals to get your dog's attention.

- Dogs primarily communicate with visual signals. Bending over in a bow, or squatting down, are visual signals that elicit dogs to approach for play, so both are effective ways of helping your pup approach.

- Dogs love to chase, and movement really catches their attention, so we'll emphasize games that get your pup running after you. These chase games teach your pup that coming is fun and exciting, and that is the key to a reliable recall ("come") later on in life.

### When and Where

- Play come games anytime, but in very short sessions; ideally, 10-20 times a day, but never do more than just a couple of repetitions at a time. Quit while she's still having a great time, before she loses interest or gets tired.

- Begin in a place with no distractions. Puppy class is not the ideal place to first try this! Try it at home without distractions for the first few weeks. Then gradually add low level distractions and play "come" games in lots of different environments. Be sure to include places that are safe but unfamiliar to her. She won't want you to get too far out of her sight. If you do this while she is young, it will have a lifelong, lasting impression on her.

- Practice off leash whenever possible (make sure it's a safe area).
- Call "Lucy, come!" when she's already heading toward you! Take advantage of these opportunities when they come up. For example, call "come" as she rushes up to get her dinner. Call "come" when she hears the leash jingle and comes racing like a bullet to the sound. Who cares why she came! You just want her to associate the sound of the word with the action of coming to you.

- Start at the beginning, not the end. Don't set your pup up to fail. For example, calling your dog to come away from company at the door or while chasing a rabbit is the astrophysics of dog training. She's just a baby, so set up situations in which she can win. And win again. She needs lots of successes to learn this well.

- Only let your pup chase you. *Never, ever chase after your pup* (no matter how much she begs you to!). She will just learn how to play "keep away" when you least want her to (like when you are late for work and need to get her in the house, and she's heading for the street).

- Only call your pup for fun and good times. During the first several months of teaching her to come, never call her for something she might think of as bad (baths, nail clipping, end of her play session, scolding her, etc.). Doing so is a surefire way to teach her not to come.

## How To Play The Game

1) Start relatively close to your puppy, about 5 feet away, or so, facing him and bending over slightly.

2) Call out his name and his come signal, then start to clap, smooch, and make silly noises. As soon as he looks at you, *immediately* run away from your puppy! The faster you run, the more encouraged he'll be to follow you.

3) As you run, continue clapping your hands. As he starts heading your way say "good dog" and continue to encourage him by running backward and clapping, whistling, smooching, and making whatever interesting noises get him excited.

Please note: the timing here is critical; say his name or "pup, pup, pup, pup" to get his attention. Say "come" just before he starts to head toward you. This is perfect timing to classically condition a stimulus and response. Don't wait until he is halfway to you to say "come;" say it just before he *begins* to move in your direction.

4) Once he has had the fun of a chase, squat down and open your arms to help direct him toward your body. If he runs past you, just get up and take off clapping while running the other way (use your voice to let him know how much fun he's missing out on!). Next time, anticipate his "zig" with your "zag." Turn the tables, play hard to get. Try to include a chase the majority of

   times that you call him. Don't be poky about it either! *Move!!* Don't underestimate the power of the chase-it's potent.

5) When he gets to you, tell him "Good," and give him glorious rewards for coming. Praise alone is just not enough to condition him to be really excited about coming to you every time you call. Your job here is to figure out exactly what will make him really glad at that moment that he came to you. Otherwise, why should he come next time when there's a cat nearby, or bunny scent on the grass? Use a variety of rewards; sometimes use his favorite food treat, other times toss the ball the instant he reaches you, or lightly "tag" him with a quick soft touch under the muzzle and immediately send him off to play! (Avoid clutching him to you in a smothering bear hug-restraint is often the last thing an excited puppy wants! So don't punish him with it if he isn't in the mood.)

Since there isn't any way to force our dogs to come from a distance our goal here is to convince our puppies that we (their humans) are the most exciting game in town.

## TEACHING METHODS

In this book you will find *"luring"* and *positive reinforcement* techniques used to teach all of the basic commands (sit, down, stand, etc.). We use these methods because they work, they are based on sound learning theory principles, and they make training *fun!*

The basic steps are:

1) First, *"lure"* or *entice* the dog into performing a behavior (preferably without touching the dog).

2) Immediately *reinforce* that behavior.

3) Later, attach a word to the behavior.

Let's apply these steps to teaching your puppy to "sit." Sitting on command is one of the most basic skills that a well mannered family dog will need to learn. Plus, it's fun and easy to do. These are the steps we'll use:

1) *"Lure"* her into a sitting position by holding food on her nose, and moving it back over her head toward her tail.

2) Immediately reinforce her as her rump touches the floor.

3) After a few sessions, say "sit" just before she begins to sit down.

## SIT

*Start out with no other distractions around.* Puppies (as well as humans!) learn best when they can concentrate on the new task without distractions.

Begin with a small, tempting, tasty treat (about the size of a raisin) to use as a "food lure." Using something soft that can be quickly eaten (like pieces of jerky-type treats, cheese, chicken, etc.) allows training to progress quickly, but pieces of kibble or biscuits can be used, if your dog loves them.

1) Holding a small piece of food between your thumb and forefinger, present it to your pup by putting it right up by her nose (within 1/2 inch). Now that you have her undivided attention, start to move your hand slowly back, between her ears towards her tail. Be careful not to pull your hand upwards. (Moving your hand upwards may make her jump up for the food.) As her nose follows the food lure back, her head should tilt up and back. As she begins to tilt her head further back in an attempt to follow the lure, her rump, by necessity, will go down to the floor.

You've just lured her into a sit. (And you didn't even need to touch her!) At the same time, she is learning to follow the movement of your hand. This will develop into a visual hand signal. Dogs are very visually oriented, so developing visual signals will be very helpful to her as you progress. Don't bother to say sit yet, you'll add that in later.

2) As her rump hits the floor, *immediately* pop that treat into her mouth! This is her reinforcement for the behavior. Don't worry about her staying in a "sit," that's the "stay" command. Right now we are just working on "sit."

A positive reinforcement is anything that makes your puppy more likely to repeat a behavior. In this case you used food to reinforce the behavior of putting her rump on the floor; of sitting. Your timing here is critical. The behavior (rump on the floor) and the reinforcement (food in this case) must be linked together in time. If you are late, you may be reinforcing a subsequent behavior (scratching her head, getting up to leave, or whatever she did after the sit). So, reinforce her *immediately* as her rump touches the floor!

3) After you can reliably elicit a sit with the food, begin to say the word "sit" (in a quiet, flat tone, no need to raise your voice) just before her rump starts to go down to the floor.

Again, your timing is important. If you want her to learn to associate the word "sit" with the behavior of putting her rump on the floor, she needs to hear the word just before she initiates the action.

Tell her what a good girl she is! Let her know you are happy with her.

Repeat steps 1 through 3 a couple more times, then stop. Puppies have very short attention spans.

## DOWN

1) Beginning with your pup in a sit, with the food lure right near his nose, slowly bring your hand straight down towards the floor. Don't pull your hand out in front of him as you do this, or he will probably stand up. Keep your hand between his front feet, while bringing it straight down. Be patient–it might take him awhile to lie down.

2) Give the treat just as his elbows touch the floor, when he's in the "down" position.

3) After your puppy lies down reliably to a lure, say "down" (in a quiet, flat or descending tone) just before he begins to lie down. Again, your timing is important. Say the command before the action, not afterwards. He will begin to associate the word "down" with the action; and that action with reinforcement.

If you are having trouble getting him to lie down, put him in a sit, and put your hand just behind his shoulders to prevent him from standing up. Be patient with your luring, sometimes it takes awhile.

Only do a few repetitions at a time. And be patient with him. It usually takes dogs a little longer to learn "down" than "sit."

### *When To Practice*
Practice sit and down in very short sessions spread throughout the day. Make it part of your normal daily routine. For example, have him lie down before you set his breakfast down; have him sit before you throw his ball; have him sit and lie down before a good romp in the yard, etc. Food isn't the only type of reinforcement! As your pup begins to get the basic idea of sit and down, practice with some distractions. This could mean another person in the room, a child playing outside, or any low level distraction. Also practice in a lot of different locations such as the living room, back yard, neighbor's yard, on the sidewalk down the block, etc.

Practice "sit" and "down" a lot in the coming week. Keep it fun and lighthearted!

# Chapter 2

# PLAY-BITING & HOUSETRAINING

**In this chapter:**

Puppy Biting.............11
Housetraining............14
Sit and Down revisited ..19
Come.....................21
Teaching Stand...........23
Socialization..............24

Good dogs have to learn how to be polite about their mouths, just as children have to learn not to slap or hit with their hands. Puppies have tiny, but very sharp teeth, as you probably have already discovered. Although those tiny teeth can really hurt sometimes, pups jaws are weak and undeveloped compared to what they will be like as adults. Puppy bites rarely cause any kind of real damage, which is exactly why this is the perfect to time to teach your pup bite inhibition.

**Bite Inhibition** is something all pups learn to some extent from their mother and siblings. As pups play with each other, one pup or another is bound to bite a litter-mate too hard. The recipient will let out a sudden, sharp "yelp" in response to the discomfort. The game suddenly ends; all play stops. With repetition puppies seem to eventually understand that a yelp meant they hurt the other party, and hurting the other party ends all the fun! Over time, through trial and error, puppies learn to play in a gentler fashion (not biting as hard) with one another so they don't loose their playmates. They learn to inhibit the force of their bites. In other words, they learn "bite inhibition."

Pups that mature without this feedback from other dogs are often unable to play politely and end up fighting instead. So bite inhibition is an essential skill that all pups need to learn as they grow up-in order to become polite members of canine society.

Since we also want our pups to be polite members of human society it is even more imperative that our pups learn finesse with their jaws near our fragile human skin. We don't have thick tough skin and fluffy fur coats to protect us from the force of canine bites!

To teach our pups not to hurt us with their teeth, we can use the same method that puppies use with one another. We'll outline a program here of systematic, progressive training that will teach your dog to use less and less force when they play bite, eventually not allowing them to mouth on people at all.

**Why go through all this?** It appears as though many of the most serious bites from adult dogs are from *dogs who never practiced with their mouths as youngsters.* They never learned how hard to bite in play or to give a warning. They always seemed to be "fine," never biting even as a puppy.

Teaching bite inhibition is a wise safety precaution that should be taken with all puppies as a general matter of course (just like getting vaccinations from the vet). It isn't much more work than just stopping all mouthing from the start, and it just *might* keep an innocent dog from getting itself into trouble someday. All dogs need to learn how to be polite family members regarding the way they use their mouths around us. Even the sweetest dog might bite if she's injured or scared.

**You are not a play toy.** Nor are your children, friends, relatives or houseguests. It's important for your pup to learn that people are not play toys or litter mates (they really don't come to us understanding this concept). Puppies need to learn that people have very fragile skin, and all human skin is to be respected, whether it's on you, or a complete stranger. This includes not only your skin, but also your hair, clothing, shoes, shoelaces, etc. If he nips your shoe, you should react the same as you would if he bit your face. Keep this in mind as you practice the steps outlined below for teaching bite inhibition.

First teach your pup to reduce the pressure of their bite, so that they apply less pressure each time they bite until they are barely touching you with their teeth. Then teach them to reduce the frequency of their mouthing on you. The goal in the end is to not allow dog teeth on human skin, at all, ever! Your puppy will learn quickly if you make it a gradual progression from one level to the next.

**Parents will need to "yelp" for young children, and perhaps even for older children.** Children's voices are often too high and too weak to impress the message on a puppy. Yelping is usually not effective for children, and may even excite the puppy to bite more. However, it often works quite well for a nearby adult to watch the child and dog (which should always be the case anyway) and yelp, "AWRP" just as the puppy's mouth is closing around the child's skin (or hair, or clothes, etc.). Then the adult or child should redirect the puppy onto an appropriate toy. Eventually, when the puppy is excited around a child he will look for the nearest toy to mouth on, instead of the child.

### *Steps To A Polite Pup*

1) The idea is to *yelp* like another puppy would. To achieve this try using the word "AWRP." It *must be sudden, abrupt, and loud*. The sound should start and stop almost instantly (no carrying on in a long drawn out death scene from "Hamlet!") from silence to full volume in a microsecond. The point is to startle your pup *just* as he bites down. (It's a good idea to practice this when your pup is not around, so you'll be good at it when you need it.) Begin by yelping only on the hardest bites, ignoring the softer bites. As you progress, yelp at gradually softer and softer pressure from your pup until he eventually mouths you with no pressure at all.

NOTE: *Don't* entice your pup to bite you. Just be ready to practice this if he initiates biting in the course of regular handling or play.

2) **Have a toy ready at all times!** Each time you enter a room pick up a dog toy, and put it in your pocket so that you are ready. After you yelp, "AWRP," the *instant* that he startles, give him the toy; wiggle it right in his face. It's crucial that the toy be presented *immediately*. The purpose of the toy is to *redirect* him onto an appropriate object. The yelp startles him and interrupts the pattern of biting on you, but redirecting him shows him what he should be doing with his mouth instead using it on you. It's important to always be giving your puppy (or your adult dog, for that matter) information about what you *do* want him to do. Show him what is acceptable (chewing on a toy rather than a human). Be sure it's a toy he really loves, perhaps a Kong™ stuffed with food?

3) Be prepared to do it again later. And again. Puppies will tend to forget themselves during the next play session and come back and bite again. Some will be very persistent about it, others will switch to a different mode more quickly. They are all individuals. Eventually though, they do get more control of themselves. It doesn't mean your puppy is mean or vicious if it takes him more time and many repetitions to get good at controlling himself, it just means you'll need to be persistent until he gets the idea.

If you try the yelping several times and find that it just gets him more excited and more mouthy, then switch gears. Try another method. Don't keep doing the same thing over and over if it's not working.

4) Another method to try, especially if he is being very persistent or if children are involved, is to dramatically jump up and leave the room in a big huff when he bites too hard. March out quickly without looking back and shut the door behind you. If your timing on this is good (it must happen quickly, the instant the bite occurs), your pup will be quite startled and dismayed that he just lost his playmate. Pups also do the equivalent of this with one another. It can be very effective with some pups. Give it a try. If the pup gets more

excited, then don't use this method. Get help from a trainer if your pup is still acting like a puppy chain saw.

By the time your pup is about 5 to 6 months old, he shouldn't be biting or mouthing on humans at all.

**Beware** of games like wrestling and roughhousing with your pup. Don't play with your pup in ways that encourage mouthing, biting and climbing on you. It can be hard to resist, but do it for your puppy's sake. It will only confuse your pup about the appropriate use of his teeth (see chapter 4 for ideas on appropriate ways to play with your pup). If you play with him in ways that involve wagging hands in his face, tempting him to bite, he'll learn that human hands are for play biting. You might not mind that, but it will confuse him when he gets in trouble for biting grandma or the little toddler down the street. He won't realize it's not okay to do the same thing with them. So don't confuse him and get him into trouble. Don't roughhouse with your pup, and don't let others do so either.

## HOUSETRAINING

Housetraining is a relatively simple concept to teach your puppy. But functionally, housetraining takes careful planning, time, and attention to details in order to pull it off quickly and efficiently. Concentrate on the details as you start this process and they will quickly become such a habit that you won't even notice the effort. Well, not too much!

### *How to do it*

Here are a few things to keep in mind about your pup in relation to housetraining.

- Up to about 12-20 weeks of age pups haven't yet developed full bladder control, so they will need to urinate at least once every hour or so that they are awake, even more frequently if they are active. It is a good idea to take them out every half hour, or more frequently, while they are awake and active. As a general rule dogs also tend to be more metabolically active first thing in the morning and again in late afternoon to evening.

- Occasionally if they are playing, chewing hard, running around, getting very excited, or generally being active in any way, they may need to go out as often as every 15 minutes.

- They will need to go out right after eating or drinking (within a few minutes after they finish).

- When they are sleeping they can wait much longer periods without needing to go outside. Don't make the mistake of thinking that just because your pup can sleep for 3 or 4 hours (or more) without needing to "go," that they can wait that long during waking periods. They can't. Dogs, like humans, are much more metabolically active when awake and moving about than when they are sleeping.

- Dogs of all ages, including puppies, do not always completely empty their bladder or bowels all at once. Some dogs do, some don't. It's not all that uncommon to have your pup "go" outside, and come in and need to "go" again 5 or 10 minutes later. In that case they probably didn't relieve themselves completely the first time. Learn your dog's natural pattern, so you aren't taken by surprise once you go back into the house. (Honest, it's just physiological, he's not deliberately trying to make your life more difficult!)

- If your pup has a tendency to do this, then you may need to spend longer outdoors, and avoid distractions until he finishes up. Then play with him and bring him in. If he won't finish his business after you've waited several mintes, bring him in, put him in his crate or room, (or stay right beside him, watching him carefully) and take him out again in 10 minutes or so, to try again. Don't give him free access to the house where he is bound to have an "accident" ("OOPS! I dropped my urine!").

## *The Logistics*

Ideally your pup should be in one of three situations at all times during this learning phase of housetraining. They should be either:

1. Outside with you.

2. Inside with your constant supervision.

3. Crated or gated off in a small, puppy-proofed room.

**1) Outside with you.** This way you are a *witness* to his activities, so you'll know for sure if he has done what he needs to do outdoors before you bring him in. Equally important is the fact that you will be there to actively train him to "go" outside.

Begin by: **a)** taking him to the area of your yard designated as his toilet area. If you always take him to this same spot, he will tend to seek out this area by choice in the future. **b)** Stand still and quietly wait until he begins to eliminate. **c)** As he *begins* to urinate quietly say the command you have chosen for this. For example, he could learn "potty" means to urinate, and "hurry up" means to defecate. (Or whatever words you have chosen) **d)** Wait quietly as he goes, and *just as he is finishing, immediately* hand him a very tasty treat, and tell him what a *very* good dog he is! Then run and play with him for a moment or two.

**2) Inside with your constant supervision.** This means you are watching him very closely (you can act as though you are doing something else, but actually you are keeping your attention on him *at all times*). You may want to attach him to you by a leash clipped to your belt. This way he can never "sneak" off to quickly "go" somewhere in your house while you're not looking.

**Beware** of those times when you are physically there with your pup, but *functionally* you are not! "Accidents" often happen when you are preoccupied with something else. You are the teacher, and therefore responsible for watching for those subtle signs that indicate that your pup may need to go outside.

**3) Crated or gated off in a small puppy proofed room.** A laundry room or kitchen, with a baby gate across the door often works well. A crate is an ideal place for a young pup under 6-12 months.

Generally dogs will try their best not to soil their sleeping area, so your pup is unlikely to soil his crate. If he does have an occasional accident, don't worry about it, just clean it up well (see below) and try to figure out why he had a problem. Was he in there too long? Did you make sure he went outside before you put him in there? Did you change his diet? You can usually figure out what the problem was. If not, a few accidents in the crate aren't a crisis. Just ignore them unless they become habitual.

**4) Other times? There are no "other" times!** For best success, and in all fairness to your pup, your puppy will simply never be allowed free, unsupervised access to your house. Period. Your pup is always in one of the three situations listed above. No exceptions.

Preventing mistakes is a very powerful training tool. Use it consistently.


## OOPS!!!

What do you do if *you* made a mistake? You got distracted, you turned your back for a moment, or for whatever reason you now find a "surprise" on your carpet? Well, if you didn't actually see the pup making the mess you're too late to do anything about it now. Don't rub your pup's nose in it, for heavens sake! Don't hit him, and don't give in to the urge to punish him in some way. After all, it was *you* that gave him the opportunity to make a mistake, wasn't it? So don't blame the puppy. Instead, put him in his crate, and clean it up.

If you do see your pup begin to squat in the house, make a loud, abrupt noise to startle him. Something as simple as a slap on a nearby wall or table can be enough to startle and interrupt your pup. Then *immediately* rush him outside (cheerfully) and give him a treat and a ton of praise for doing it out there. Come back in, and put him in his crate for a moment while you clean up his "accident."

Remember that the goal is to *startle* him to *interrupt* the behavior of soiling the floor indoors, not to punish him. Being very harsh with him or punishing the mistake will only help him learn that he shouldn't do it while you are watching. So logically, being the intelligent chap that he is, next time he'll have enough sense to sneak off somewhere and do it while you aren't looking. What's more, he might not "go" when outside on walks anymore, because you are there, and he has learned that you get crazy when he goes potty!

## Clean Up

How you clean up "accidents" in the house is crucial. If you don't remove the source of the odor completely, it will attract your dog back to that spot like a neon sign saying "*Public Restroom-Potty Here!!*"

Don't use vinegar or household cleaners. Most cleaners contain ammonia, the scent of which will attract your dog back to that location, just as the scent of his own urine would. Instead use a commercial, enzymatic cleaner designed especially for this purpose (like Nature's Miracle or Outright, to name just a few). Properly used, it will remove the source of the odor so your pup won't be attracted to that particular spot again. In a pinch, you can use baking soda or club soda to neutralize the odor.

## Reading Your Pup's Signals

It's crucial that you observe your puppy and learn to read his signals. Some signals he may give that indicate he needs to go out are:

- Your pup just woke up.

- He just ate or drank.

- You just greeted him and released him from confinement, (he is excited).

- He is wandering away from an area he was playing in, or his eating or sleeping area.

- He is sniffing the floor.

- He's circling while sniffing.

- He might be looking a bit confused or distracted from what he was doing.

- He might be looking in the direction of the door he usually goes out, or pacing or wandering into that area.

- Or, he might be wandering over to an area he has soiled before, especially if he starts sniffing in that area.

- Be suspicious of any pacing or whining that doesn't seem to have a specific purpose.

- If he was playing hard (especially if he was playing with another dog or a human) and he hasn't been out for awhile. Sometimes pups can get so busy playing they don't take out time to go find a spot, they just squat in mid-romp! Avoid this by interrupting hard, prolonged play sessions with potty breaks.

- You see him begin to squat.

- Or any number of other, individual clues that he is about to "go." It's important for you to be very observant and learn to recognize and notice your own pup's particular behavior patterns.

## *More Freedom In The House*

The key to success in introducing your pup to new rooms of your house is to take this one step at a time, very slowly and in a very controlled manner.

Dogs can learn to be very reliable in all rooms of the house if they are introduced to them one at a time, with you there constantly supervising. When you first start to allow a pup into a new room he won't realize this is part of the family "den," and therefore won't realize he needs to keep it clean. That's where your careful planning and supervision comes in.

Take him into the new room after he has gone outside and you are certain he won't need to "go" for awhile. Sit in that room with him for awhile, perhaps with him tied to you by a leash. Sit on the floor and read a book, or do some other activity that allows you to keep some of your attention on your pup. Pet him and talk to him occasionally. If he falls asleep by your side all the better. Feed him his dinner in that room. Play with him in that room. Do some training with him in that room. Spend some time in there every day. After many exposures to that room, under these controlled conditions, he will begin to realize that this room is also part of his "den" (a sleeping, eating, and living space) and he will do his best to keep it clean.
This process of assimilation and understanding can take awhile for your pup, so don't try to rush it. Introduce each room in your house one at a time, carefully. If he is doing very well in there you can begin to leave him in there for short moments, while you peek in from around the corner. Start with brief test periods, and gradually allow him longer access to the room without you (do continue to watch him from a distance or from around the corner).

If he starts to make a mistake, startle him, take him out, clean it up, and then go back to close, strict supervision. It means he isn't ready for that much freedom yet. Be patient, eventually you'll be able to give him run of the house with peace of mind.

## Problems?

If at any point you find your pup regressing and making mistakes-mistakes you thought he was past making-don't despair! This is common and nothing to worry about. Although it may be a bit frustrating for you, try to relax and just help your pup get it right by backing up in your training.

Go back to taking him out more, watching him more closely, and confining him more judiciously when you can't keep your attention on him. Basically, go back to the beginning and start teaching him again. It won't take nearly as long the second time around (or third time). Also look at how fast you were progressing; perhaps it was too fast for him to get a thorough understanding of what he needed to learn. Have faith! It will come with time.

**One last word of advice:** if your pup seems to be urinating more often than normal or having a lot of trouble with the housetraining, go see your veterinarian to rule out health problems. Dogs can get urinary tract infections just like people do, and it may be causing him to have trouble controlling his bladder. This is more common in females than males, but it can happen with both sexes. There can also be other medical reasons for urinary incontinence, so check out his health if you have any doubts about it at all.

## SIT AND DOWN REVISITED

### Visual Hand Signals

The luring motion that you have been doing with your hand to elicit the sit or down position is already the beginning of a visual *cue* or *signal*. Since dogs communicate primarily visually, it is easy to imagine how important visual cues can be to your dog. Visual hand signals will help your dog understand what you want.

Remember, that "sit" is generally easier for most dogs than "down" is, so be ready to give him more help with the "down" command. Give him clear verbal and visual cues. You may also need to keep using a food lure longer with the "down" command than with "sit," especially if there are distractions around.

After luring him into a sit one or two times, try using the same hand movements you used to get your pup to sit or lie down without any food in your hand. Just pretend the food is there. Move your hand to lure your dog into a sit, and quickly rub his chest (avoid patting the top of his head when reinforcing him, dogs usually aren't too fond of that!) and praise him like he had just won the lottery for you! Then try it again without any food lure, but produce a treat out of your opposite hand (yes, you *were* keeping the treat hidden.) to reinforce him once he sits or lies down.

As your pup catches on to this (usually very quickly), your hand movement can become more of an upward sweep (palm up) for "sit," and a downward sweep (palm down to the floor) for "down."

## Verbal Signals

Be sure to say your signal the same way every time. Don't say "down" one day and "lie down" the next. Also guard against using "down" in different contexts, like when he jumps on the couch. That will just make it harder for him to learn what down means.

## Intermittent Reinforcement

It's crucial when using food (or any reinforcer) to switch over to a schedule of *intermittent reinforcement* once your pup is reliably producing the behavior that you are teaching. In this case, if luring your pup with your hand and/or a treat is consistently producing a sit or down then it's time to move on to intermittent reinforcement.

The dictionary describes "intermittent" as *"ceasing at intervals."* This is a helpful way to think of it. It doesn't say "stopping altogether"! So don't be too anxious to think that "less-is-better" to the point of not giving any treats at all. You might loose the "sit" and "down" that you have so far. Instead, continue to give a treat (or toy, or belly rub, or ball toss, etc.) the majority of times.

**Start to reinforce only the better "sits" and "downs."** For example, reinforce only the ones that happen fastest, or the ones where he is being most attentive to you. Don't reward the slower, sloppier ones at all. This serves a double benefit: you are making the reinforcements intermittent, which will strengthen the behavior (he will actually work harder for a reinforcement if he isn't quite sure when or if he might get one). And, you are also letting him know which types of sits or downs that you like best (quick, attentive ones). He will soon figure out that he gets the treat for the quick sit, and nothing for the sit that you had to coax out of him.

When using a treat as a reinforcement, begin to surprise your pup with it. *Keep him guessing!* Make him wonder "does my owner have a treat for me this time? Even if I know he has food on him/her, does that mean he/she will give it to me this time?" (Yes it's true! Even if you do have treats on you, that doesn't mean you always have to give one to your pup!)

At this point continue to give the reinforcement the majority of the time, but not always. Bring food treats out of your other hand, or your pocket. Begin to phase out using the food as a lure, and mostly just save it as a reinforcement. You want your pup to learn to listen to your voice command, and watch for your visual hand signals even when the food is not in sight.

## Vary The Reinforcers

Make a point of beginning to use other types of reinforcements besides food, if you haven't already. If you are integrating training into your daily routine you will have plenty of opportunities to use real life reinforcements. This is another way to begin cutting back on the amount of food used as reinforcements.

**Anything your pup wants at the moment can be a reinforcement.** Does he want you to throw the ball for him? Great, then ask him to sit, and the *instant* his rump hits the floor, throw that ball immediately! Does he want his dinner? Ask for a quick "sit" and "lie down," and as his elbows touch the floor put his food in front of him (and give him lots of calm, warm praise as he eats).

**Use food less and less, and other reinforcements more and more!**

## Finding Time To Train Your Pup

Continue to work in lots of short sessions scattered throughout your day. Not only does your pup learn best this way, it also makes it easy for you to fit it in. It may be hard to come up with half an hour at a time to train your pup, but it's easy to fit in 30 seconds or a minute here and there throughout your day. It also helps your pup learn that obedience is just a fun, natural part of life. It becomes second nature to him-a habit-which will make it easier for him to consistently obey you.

# COME

If you've been practicing "come" with your pup as suggested, he should be starting to really think of "come" as a game. He'll be much more likely to come to you now. You've made yourself interesting to him and the source of this great game. Good job!

Continue to play chase games, clapping your hands and calling your pup energetically as he runs toward you. Run away from him. Zig and zag. Play hard to get. Add some variations: drop to the floor when he gets near you, and let him lick your face (no biting). Or throw a toy behind you, so he goes racing after it just when he thought you were done! Scratch his chin, and gently take his collar while giving him a treat, then immediately release him to go play again. Or better yet, immediately go running off so he can chase you again. Sometime when he thinks you're all done playing, surprise him by taking him inside, and immediately release him back outside to play some more! Use a wide variety of reinforcements. Be creative, your dog will love you for it.

If he's having any trouble with "come," then decrease the number of nearby distractions while you are practicing, and increase the level of reinforcement. Figure out what he really, really loves most, and use it. Don't worry if it's silly, dogs seem to love silly! After all, isn't one of a dog's main functions in life to remind us what being silly and light hearted is all about?

**Only call your pup for fun and good times. Remember not to call him to "come" for something he might perceive as bad.** If that's the case, go get him. Don't misuse his trust by calling him (just because it is more convenient for you) to put him away while you go out for several hours; or by calling him to take something away from him, or to force him to visit with someone he's afraid of, etc. He may come this time, he may even come several times, but eventually he'll figure out that it's not a good idea to come to you when you call. Ignoring you will be tempting enough for him as he reaches adolescence, no need to get started early! So be careful to build that strong, positive association in his mind, between "come" and a wonderful time. Do it *now,* while he's really primed for it.

### Hide and Seek

Hide and seek is a wonderful game for helping your pup learn to pay attention to where you are at all times. It also teaches your pup to come find you when you call, even if you are out of sight. All well-mannered adult dogs should keep some part of their attention on their owner. Hide and seek is a great way to start developing that habit in your pup.

**Take your pup to a new location**, someplace safe, preferably fenced. Play with your pup for awhile, then wait around until he gets bored and starts exploring the area on his own. Sneak behind a tree, bush, bench, around the corner of a building or whatever is handy, to hide. Hide somewhere that allows you to peek out and keep an eye on him, without letting him see you.

Eventually he will bring his nose up off the ground for some air. When he looks around and realizes that he has "lost" you, he'll look a little worried. Make some little noise, from your hiding spot, until his head gets directed generally toward you. Then try being quiet again. Let him worry a little and let him do the work of finding you. After all, he's the one that lost you, not vice versa! Make another little noise if he gets way off track.

When he does find you, squeal with delight and go running off, letting him chase you around the tree or bush, or drop onto the ground and give him a big belly rub and lots of praise. Then go running off and hide again! This time call him as you run off, then dart behind a bush or tree. It doesn't matter if you're not completely hidden, he'll still have fun finding you. Once your pup figures out this is a fun game, he will try to watch you more closely, so he can win.

Try it at home, indoors. It's a good way to keep his mind and body exercised on stormy days. Have someone hold him while you hide just a few feet away. Make it easy for him at first. You'll quickly reach the point where he'll find you anywhere in your house or yard.

But do remember to also try it in unfamiliar places away from home. That will have the biggest impact toward making him realize he can't afford to lose you out there in that big wide world. So he'd better start keeping better track of where you are. After all, humans get lost *so* easily!

Keep on working on "come." It takes months of fun practice to get a reliable "come," but it's worth every minute later on. Concentrate right now on making him *really* enjoy that word!

### *Expanding Your Puppy's Repertoire*
**The more commands he knows, the easier it is to teach him new ones,** because he has learned how to learn. And remember his entire nervous system is geared up for learning right now. In fact, he is constantly learning all the time. So this is the perfect opportunity to have him learn *useful* and *acceptable* behaviors *you* have chosen rather than some of the things he could be coming up with on his own.

In addition, as he learns various commands they can be used to distract and redirect him when he's getting himself into trouble. For example: perhaps he's barking at a dog going by while you are out on your walk. Instead of letting him get himself carried away with this unacceptable behavior, give him some familiar behaviors to do instead, to occupy his mind and body. Have him sit, down, stand, down, sit, or some variation on that theme. Then resume your walk. That's a lot for a young pup, but you'll find the technique helpful, especially as he gets older and reaches adolescence. You are building the foundation now for a broad set of basic commands to have at your disposal later.

## STAND
Stand is a handy command for family dogs to know. Combined with stay, which is introduced in a later chapter, you can use it to get him to stand still while you wipe muddy paws. Or it can make it easier for the veterinarian to examine him, or for you to groom him. It can even make it easier for you to take his picture!

**To teach stand:**
1) Use a food lure to teach the new command, "stand." Begin with your pup in a sit. Put the food right near his nose. Pull your hand *slowly out in a straight line*

*away from your puppy's nose.* Don't pull your hand upward or downward as you do this, but keep it on a level plane with his nose, parallel to the floor. Bring it straight out in front of him. If his nose follows the food he will have to stand up in order to stay near it as it moves.

2) Say "stand" *just before he initiates the action.*

3) Pop the treat in his mouth just as he *stands up.*

Practice a couple times and quit. Practice again later. Teach stand in short little micro sessions just like your other commands.

Remember this is a new command for him, so at first you will need to give him the food lure as a reinforcement each and every time he stands up. Once you see that he seems to be catching on (he does the stand reliably and consistently with the lure), then and only then, begin to give the reinforcement intermittently ("ceasing at intervals"). Also start to phase out the food lure. Make the same motion but without the food between your fingers.

## Visual Signal for Stand
Try a level swing of your hand with your palm flat, facing the floor, moving away from your pup's face.

Also practice getting him to stand from a down position, using the same technique described for getting him to stand from a sit.

## Socialization
**Keep on socializing that puppy!** He needs lots of positive experiences out there in the world with all kinds of people, dogs, other animals, objects, sounds, sights, smells, and so on.

That's what socializing is; exposing him in a positive way to the world he'll live in and the things he'll encounter as he grows up.

Do it now while it will have the most impact on him. And keep on socializing him throughout his life, but especially during the whole first year of his life.

# Chapter 3

# VERBAL PRAISE & CORRECTIONS

**In this chapter:**

*Verbal Praise* .............*25*
*Corrections*................*26*
*Sit-Down-Stand*..........*30*
*Come* .....................*31*
*Walking by your side* ....*32*
*"Belly Up" or*
   *"Play Dead"*.........*35*

Good dog! It sounds obvious doesn't it? It's easy to fall into the trap of thinking our dogs should automatically understand what those words mean. After all, we do. But the fact is our pups don't come into this world understanding English, and that includes phrases like "Good dog!"

If our intent is to make our dogs feel good and let them know we are happy with them, then it's important to make sure they truly understand what "Good dog" means. But for too many dogs "Good dog" is just a vaguely familiar phrase without much specific meaning.

If our praise doesn't really make our dogs feel good, then it's not going to be effective as a reinforcement.

Although many dogs do pick up the intent of our praise to some extent, it works best if we consciously and deliberately condition our puppies to associate our praise with something pleasant and meaningful to them.

**You can condition your puppy to enjoy your praise by saying "Good dog"** (or your favorite praise words) **when he is already feeling good.** For example, say "Gooood dog!" in a relatively low, quiet voice, and warm, friendly tone:

- As you give him treats during training.
- As he enjoys his dinner.
- When he's chewing on a wonderful new toy.
- When he's getting a belly rub and blissfully savoring every second of it!

- As he greets you, wiggling his body and tail from the shoulders back.

- As he's drifting off to sleep on a full belly, cuddling by you contentedly.

- As he's playing nicely with another dog and having a great time.

- Anytime he's feeling really good (and not getting into mischief at the same time!)

**Eventually an association will form in your pup's mind between the sound of your praise and feeling good.** He will begin to seek out your praise because it is important and relevant to him; it has the power to make him feel good!


## CORRECTIONS

"No" is another human word that does not come hardwired in your puppy's brain. Again, it's a word that puppies need to learn, just like any other word.

A puppy's full time occupation is learning about the environment she lives in. Puppies are constantly learning, constantly exploring their environment. This means they are bound to get into things they shouldn't, sooner or later! How you react when your pup gets into mischief will determine how quickly she learns the rules about what is (or is not) acceptable. Your reactions can also effect how much she will trust you.

**Corrections can be informative and help your puppy learn boundaries. Punishments tend to confuse and frighten puppies (and adult dogs as well).**

A good correction *startles* your puppy and *interrupts* the behavior *at the moment that it is happening,* so you can redirect her towards something more appropriate.

A good correction gives her feedback that helps her learn without frightening or hurting her.

In contrast, punishment takes place *after* the fact, and is usually punitive without much helpful information coming from it. Punishment tends to just frighten or hurt, but *not effectively inform* your pup about what she did wrong, or how she might get it right next time. Let's look at a couple of examples of both:

**Example # 1:** Riley is a normal 11 week old puppy; active, inquisitive, and curious. She explores and investigates her world with her teeth, just as all puppies do. One day Riley notices a small plastic object sitting on a low table in the family room. Everyone in the family handles this little item often and it smells like Mom, Dad, and the kids. Since this little "toy" is right at nose level, in easy reach and it smells great, Riley grabs the remote control off the table to play with it.

After Riley chews on it for a few moments, Mom suddenly yells and charges at Riley, grabbing her suddenly, scolding her with a harsh tone and yanking her around roughly by the collar. Mom yanks the "toy" out of Riley's mouth and abruptly shoves her in her crate, swatting Riley's rump just before closing the door. Riley is confused, frightened, and not really quite sure what just transpired. Mom isn't usually like that, and it was kind of scary.

A few days later, Riley finds the remote control on the floor near the sofa where one of the kids left it. The little "toy" even smells like the butter Joey had on his fingers from eating popcorn. Riley can't resist! She lies down and begins licking, then chewing on the crunchy little plastic thing. After awhile Riley gets distracted and runs off to see what smells good in the kitchen. (This time Riley got away with chewing on the remote, so most likely she will think it was O.K. to do so.)

Later, Dad notices the chewed up remote control, and throws an absolute fit. He yells angrily at Riley to "come here right now!" grabbing Riley by the scruff of the neck and shaking her hard. He even slaps Riley's mouth as he waves the remote control in Riley's face. Finally Dad grabs Riley up roughly and shoves her in her crate. Dad seems awfully mad. But why? Riley hasn't a clue.

**What did Riley learn here?** She learns to head the other way when she hears "Come," because coming to her family is sometimes frightening or painful. She'll learn to play "keep away from the human" whenever she has a really *prize* possession in her mouth. Riley learned that human hands can hurt her and should be avoided. She may learn to growl at people to guard her "treasures," since people only reach for them to steal them away. She will probably never quite trust Mom or Dad (and possibly other humans) since they seem unpredictable and dangerous at times. Finally, Riley learned that her crate is not necessarily such a good place after all.

Lets look at another example that begins with the same set of circumstances, but has a very different outcome.

**Example # 2:** Tasha is a normal, active, inquisitive, 11-week-old pup. Tasha's family "puppy-proofed" the house and provided Tasha with lots of exciting toys. Tasha never gets lonely or bored in the family room, because a family member is always with Tasha whenever she is in that room. They watch her and play with her and take her out often. They provide lots of toys and chewy things for Tasha to bite on.

The first time Tasha noticed the remote control on the coffee table, with its easy access, good smells, and fun little buttons all over it, Mom noticed it too. Mom, being wise to the ways of puppies, put it up out of Tasha's reach. Then she redirected Tasha to her wonderful, chewy Kong™ toy which she wiggled around and threw a few feet away. Tasha couldn't resist chasing it and immediately forgot the remote control.

A few days later when the remote control was on the floor covered with the smell of butter, Tasha decided it must be for her. As she was about to pick it up, she heard Dad (from around the corner) say "Ah" in an abrupt, deep warning tone. Just then a loud "whack" thumped beside Tasha as a paperback book fell out of the sky, landing right beside her! Tasha was so startled, she forgot about the remote control as she ran to Dad who was calling her to safety near him. Dad had a terrific tennis ball ready which he threw across the kitchen floor, just to help Tasha find something safer to play with than that nasty old remote control!

Over the following weeks Mom and Dad made sure that the remote control was either picked up out of Tasha's reach *at all times,* or that the sky or the floor "exploded" around her whenever Tasha tried to help herself to the remote control (they had "set-ups" prepared to startle her if she tried to take the remote).

**What did Tasha learn here?** First of all that people are a safe haven when scary things happen: so "run towards your family if things are scary, rather than running away from them!" Tasha believed the environment itself corrected her, so she will eventually decide to leave that remote control alone, whether anyone is watching her or not. Tasha has learned that remote controls are really not worth the trouble, even when they smell like butter. Tasha learned there are lots of fun things to do and to play with other than that icky remote control. She also learned that Mom and Dad warn Tasha of danger with the word "Ah" or "No," so she will try to pay close attention when she hears that warning sound.

Tasha is on her way to establishing some really good habits that will serve her well, and make her a well mannered family dog. She is getting clear, instructive feedback from her environment and helpful guidance from her owners (rather than learning to fear and mistrust them). She will figure out the "rules" to living in her family's house quickly. She will make plenty of mistakes, as all youngster do, but she will learn useful and productive lessons from her mistakes, while building a trusting bond with her family.

What are the keys to helping your pup learn her boundaries within human society?

## 1) Set Rules
**Decide what your family rules will be, and enlist the whole family to work together as a team to consistently maintain those rules.** If Dad lets Ginger bite and wrestle, Ginger won't understand she's not suppose to do the same with Grandma or little Susie. If Grandma lets Ginger cuddle next to her on the couch any time she wants, Ginger won't understand why Mom is always getting angry with her for jumping up in Mom's lap when she sits down. Have clearly defined family rules concerning the puppy so that you don't confuse her.

## 2) Prevention and Supervision
**Don't give your puppy opportunities to learn bad habits.** This can't be emphasized enough. Puppy-proof your home and supervise your puppy until she learns the rules. Eventually she will learn how to be good without supervision, but that will take many months of guidance and training. You wouldn't leave a toddler alone in a room without guidance, would you? Well, your pup has just as much to learn about how to be safe and how to be "good" as a human child does, so don't set her up to fail. Prevent mishaps before they happen.

## 3) Remote Corrections and "Set-ups"
**A "remote" correction is one that occurs independently of you being near the puppy.** It can be anything that startles and interrupts the puppy from whatever she was doing. It could be a slap against the wall (just to make a noise). Or it could be a paperback book, an empty pop can (with a few pebbles in it, with the top taped shut), or a bean bag, tossed on the floor near the pup. The point is to toss it *near* her to *startle* her, not to hit her with it. Say "Ah" or "No" just before it hits the floor so your pup learns that your word is a warning. Eventually your verbal warning will be enough.

**A "set-up" is similar in that it does not seem to be connected to you.** Cookie sheets (lightweight aluminum ones) and empty pop cans work well for many things. For example, if you want to teach your pup not to steal food off the coffee table, put out a tempting piece of food, with the cookie sheet and pop cans carefully balanced on the table so as to fall at the slightest touch of the food. When your pup tries to steal the food (which you could also soak in bitter apple or a similar distasteful product) the whole works will tip and come tumbling down around her ears! With just a couple repetitions most puppies will get the idea that the table "explodes" whenever she puts her head or feet on it.

Get creative and think of ways to get the environment to correct her when possible. Just make sure your solutions won't hurt her or terrify her. *Keep in mind that what startles one puppy is fun for another, so customize your set-up for your own pup.*

## 4) Redirection
**Startling your pup with a remote correction is only part of your job.** It's vital that you *constantly* show her what she should be doing instead. *Redirect* her to a toy or to another activity. Or ask her to do some commands like "sit," "down," "stand," or "come" (or several of them combined).

Show her what some other options are besides the behavior that got her into trouble. Over time she will eventually learn that she has other options, and she will begin to make better choices.

## 5. Physical Corrections Should be Rare
**Although you may need to physically correct your pup at some point (or points) in her life, those occasions should be extremely *rare*.** They should *not* be a routine part of your pup's education. If they are, seek out a good trainer and/or behaviorist to help you get your relationship with your dog back on track. Frequent physical corrections indicate a lack of communication and understanding between you and your canine pupil.

All corrections should have certain qualities to be effective:

- First of all, corrections should not involve anger. Corrections are to teach and educate your pup. How well do you learn when someone is angrily screaming in your face or hitting you?

- Secondly, a good physical correction should be clear enough, and firm enough so that the pup is absolutely clear that this is a correction and not confuse it with play. But it should not be so strong as to terrify or hurt your pup. "Remote" corrections (what you use 100% of the time with most pups, 99% of the time with others) only need to be *startling*. They *don't* need to frighten her to be effective. They only need to interrupt her current behavior, so you can redirect her to a more acceptable behavior.

- Thirdly, both types of corrections should happen almost at the speed of light. A correction should be over with almost as soon as it starts.

- **The timing of your correction is critical.** Corrections should happen slightly before or just as the pup gets into trouble (just as she initiates the undesirable behavior). Just as quickly, you should be showing her what an appropriate alternative behavior is. So immediately redirect your pup with a toy, some commands, or another activity (or to another area).

## SIT-DOWN-STAND
If you've been practicing these commands with your pup, he should be doing them reliably most of the time, if there are no distractions. When practicing these commands in familiar places with few distractions, be sure to use treats less and less, substituting praise, toys, and chest rubs for food.

**Begin to add in distractions gradually.** Some things that can be considered mild distractions would be: practicing outside instead of inside; training with the cat waiting by the doorway; or, practicing with new people watching.

Any small change of noise, movement, smell, presence of others, or change of location (context) can be considered a distraction. We wouldn't expect a puppy who has been practicing quietly in the house without the cat around to "down" while two cats chase each other through the room! That would be too much to ask of the pup all at once. Your pup will eventually get to that point, but you will need to help him get there step by step. Don't expect your puppy to jump from step 2 or 3 to step 25 without working up to it gradually.

Begin to practice "sit" and "down" using *just your verbal command* (no hand signal, and no lure) or *just your visual signal* (no voice). It's good practice for him, and it will be informative to see which aspects of your commands are effective. Does he notice your voice the most, or your visual signals more? Practice using each type of signal (verbal or visual) alone until he's good at both individually.

**Be sure you are also using a variety of reinforcements.** Food treats are just one way to reinforce your pup, be sure to find lots and lots of other ways to reinforce him (like chase-his-human games, balls, Kongs™, dinner, going outside, walks, belly rubs, releasing him to go play with another dog, etc.).

## COME

Practice "come"...*always!!* Continue to make "come" a fun game. Call your puppy to you often, then *immediately release* her to go do something else fun. Take advantage of times when she is racing joyously to you of her own accord (you just got the leash out of the closet; you're pulling her "lost" toy out from under the couch; etc.). Call "come" just before she starts to head your way. Don't call her to "come" too many times in a row. Call her once or twice (3 or 4 times at the most), *and always make it worth her while,* then quit. Do this several times a day, in all different locations indoors and out, on leash and off leash (in safe places).

Remember not to call your pup for things she perceives as "bad." That's a surefire way to teach her *not* to come.

**Only use this command when you are willing to go and get your pup if she doesn't come.** And don't stand there repeatedly telling her to "come" when she is totally enthralled in some major distraction. If she's rolling in her first cow pie, what do think the chances are that she'll leave it to come to you? About zero! So don't call her to "come" when you know she's not going to do it. Otherwise she'll just learn to ignore that empty chatter you keep rattling off ("come puppy, come, come, come") while she heads the other way.

Instead, go get her. If she doesn't come, don't reel her in like a fish on a line, or punish her, but do be *persistent* and interesting enough to draw her attention back onto you.

**If you have already called "come," be sure you get her to come to you. Don't give up.** Don't let her learn that she can ignore your request. Quietly walk up to her, and from about 2 inches in front of her nose, call, clap, whistle, laugh, squeak, smooch, play bow, wave a piece of food or a toy (then put it back in your pocket, you don't want to bribe her, just get her attention), or whatever works. Make some variety of playful noises that get her attention, then lure her away.

Once you get her started, take off running! Move! Find some way to get her attention on you, and get her following you, if only for a couple of feet. Then give her something better than what she just left. Better yet, if at all possible *release her to go back to the distraction she just left* (you're going to have to bathe her anyway, you might as well get some heavy duty training leverage out of that disgusting cow pie incident!)

Begin to add some mild distractions when you call her to "come." Build up your distraction level gradually. You want her to learn to pay attention to you when other things are going on around her, but you don't want to lose her attention altogether. And you will lose her attention if you expect too much of her too quickly.

Instead, add distractions a bit at a time. If what you added was too much for her, and you completely lost her attention, try again with less distractions and better reinforcements. Then try going back to your original distraction, but call her from a much shorter distance away, giving her a *lot more help* this time around.

Remember, your puppy will learn best by repeated successes. So stretch the envelope a bit, ask for a bit more, make your requests a little bit more challenging for her, but help her to *succeed*.


## WALKING BY YOUR SIDE

When puppies are young they have a strong social attachment to their caregivers. This means they don't want you to get too far out of their sight (this is why "hide and seek" in strange new places makes such a powerful impression on puppies at this age). You can use this *social attachment* to help *condition* your pup to love being next to you as you walk. A more formal "heel" command will come later. For now your objective is to motivate your puppy to *want* to keep up with you and walk by your side. At this stage you are helping your pup develop the *habit* of keeping an eye on you and staying close by as you move around.

Since there are lots of tempting and distracting things out there in the world, *you will need to be really fun and exciting to keep your pup focused on you,* rather than all those worldly distractions.

**Your goal is to be so captivating to your pup that she will be glad she noticed you!!**

## Off Leash "Following" Game

1) Begin in a safe, quiet, but unfamiliar place (unfamiliar to your pup), *without* distractions. You don't need a leash if your pup is under three months or is relatively "clingy." If your pup is getting more independent, let a leash drag behind her or do this in a fenced yard-*safety first!* Set her down and slap the side of your left leg as you trot off. She'll scramble to keep up with you, especially if you make little smooching or clicking noises with your tongue.

2) After she has followed you for a few steps, turn and take off in another direction. Slap the side of your left leg as you take off (don't completely outrun her though!). Smooch, click, do *something* to get her attention in a fun, playful way. As she catches up to your left side, give her some kind of reinforcement that she really loves-a food treat, a squeaky toy, a tennis ball, etc. Make sure she is *really glad* to be there by your side.

3) Then jog, dash, skip, run, scramble, or trot off again! After she gets to chase you a little bit, reinforce her for catching up with you, then continue treating her as she follows by your side.

**Repeat this game just a few times and then quit while you are both still having lots of fun.** Do it again later in the day. Practice this in your house, your yard, for 30 seconds in the middle of you walks, etc. Practice it often throughout the day in little 10 second bursts. Be sure to try it often in unfamiliar places while she is still young. You'll make the biggest impression on her when you do it away from home where she may be a bit more concerned about "losing" you.

**The key to making this work well (conditioning her to think that walking with her human is a blast.) is to be totally unpredictable and erratic.** If you keep her fascinated and wondering what in the world you'll do next, you'll earn her undivided attention.

**Reinforce her often for being next to you as you are moving.** Walking by your side in a heel position takes some concentration for your pup. It doesn't seem to be a natural position for dogs. If you watch a pack of dogs or wolves walking together, they don't tend to "heel" to one another. They are constantly shifting about in front, behind, off to the sides. Heeling doesn't seem to be part of a dog's natural repertoire, so expect it to take some time … and lots of help from you. A flashy heel can easily take a year to teach, so be patient. Practice this following game in very, very short sessions at first. Puppies will tire out or lose concentration quickly, so do a few short, peppy spurts (maybe 3 to 5 seconds long at first), and then quit for awhile, and do it again later in the day.

You'll notice at this point we haven't put a word on this position yet. It's a good idea to get the behavior working fairly well before you put a name on it.

As you do start to put a name on it, you might want to choose a casual name that means polite walking next to you, and save the word "heel" for a more formal command later. (Heel traditionally means a very specific position with the dog's neck next to your left leg-not further ahead or behind by more than a couple inches. It's a much more precise, more advanced concept for her to learn.)

Whatever word you use, *say it when she is in the correct position*. Don't say it while she's behind you, forging ahead of you, or heading off in a beeline away from you! *Only say your command* ("let's go," "follow me," "walk nicely," "left side," "over here," "walk politely," etc.) *just before she moves into that position*. You're not going to want her to associate "walk politely" with the action of darting off after a squirrel!

## Walking Politely on Leash

Everyone's seen them-the Suburban sled dogs, from 5 pounds to 205 pounds-hauling their owners down the street from light post to tree to bush to fire hydrant. Do you know how they teach sled dogs and carting dogs to pull heavy loads (the dogs that really *are* suppose to put all their weight into pulling)? They put a slow, gradually increasing resistance at the other end of the dog's leash. A dog's muscles are designed to actually resist, or pull against, a slow steady pressure on them.

What this means for the average puppy owner trying to walk the family dog around the neighborhood is that the more that the leash tightens up, the harder the dog will pull against it in the opposite direction.

Since dogs are considerably stronger than humans, pound for pound, your dog will be practically pulling you right off your feet before he is even full grown. Regardless of your dog's size, your cute little pup will be doing the same thing to you soon if you don't prevent this habit from starting. As with most bad habits, it's always easier to prevent it from starting than to have to "fix" it once it has been learned.

How can you prevent this habit from developing in your pup? Simply put, never let him pull on leash. But how, you ask?! *Turn around. Turn around 180° every time you feel that leash tightening.* Start now, today. Take off walking in the opposite direction of his pulling. Be interesting, be erratic, slap your leg, give him some pleasant reason to pay attention to you, coo at him, make funny faces at him, and reinforce him as he catches up to your side.

If he forges ahead again, just turn 180° again, and reinforce him as he catches up once more. You may have to turn every few steps at first, but it *will* get better. Don't shout at him or fling him around by the neck. Just let him know through your actions (turning 180°) *that you will consistently put yourself back in the lead.* Let him figure out that he doesn't get very far when he tries to initiate the speed and direction of your walk, but if he'll follow your lead, he'll have a good time and you'll keep him moving.

## BELLY UP (PLAY DEAD)

Since it is wise to be constantly expanding your puppies repertoire, the classic "play dead" command is a fun behavior to teach your pup. It can be very handy for grooming or when the veterinarian needs to examine your pup. It's also a cute trick for impressing visitors. *To teach "Belly up:"*

- Begin with your pup in the "down" position. Using a smelly, tasty treat, lure your pup's nose *slowly* down toward her side, moving your hand in a half-circle down toward the ground and then upward and backward toward her hip. If her head stops, move your hand back to her nose, and begin again. You might have gone too fast the first time.

- Continue to lure her head back toward her hip which will cause her weight to shift to the opposite hip. Continue luring over the hip, until she flops onto her back.

- Give her the treat *instantly* as she flops onto her back. Say "Belly up" (or "Play dead," or "Sleepy dog," etc.) at the same time.

### Roll Over

For *"Roll Over,"* begin from the "Belly up" position. Move your lure from his nose, to the floor on his *opposite* side. If his head follows the lure, his body will follow and he should flip over into a complete "Roll over." Give the treat just as he flops over into the finished position.

# Chapter 4

# PLAY

**In this chapter:**
*Play while training* .......*37*
*When play backfires* ......*43*
*Stealing* ....................*45*

**P**uppies learn a lot about their environment through play. Play helps them sort out social hierarchy issues, figure out their physical limitations, and helps them gain confidence in their abilities. Play helps puppies bond to their littermates and other companions and helps them bond to their new human families as well.

## *Play While Training and Train While Playing.*

Puppies need to learn the rules of any games they play, just as human children do. When children play games like softball, they have to learn how to play within the boundaries of the rules that govern the game. Puppies, like children, don't seem to mind learning the rules if they enjoy the game. So just as obedience is not a form of punishment or discipline, neither should play be completely unrestrained, wild, rowdy behavior without any limits.

Obedience should be integrated into your pup's play, and play can be very useful when integrated into obedience. The two should be part and parcel of one another. Play helps motivate your puppy and keep him interested in what you are doing. It's a very effective training tool, and it's always readily available. Professional trainers often use play to produce reliable results when training dogs for the Obedience ring, Schutzhund, or Search and Rescue work. Even police dogs are often trained to a very high level of reliability using play as the motivating factor. So don't underestimate the power of play as a motivator to produce a well mannered family dog that *wants* to do as you ask.

There are a lot of games that are constructive and fun for your pup to learn. Here are some ideas to get you started.

## *"Take it" and "Drop it"*

One of the first things to teach your pup is how to give you the toy (or remote control, or your best shoes) that she has in her mouth.

Begin with a toy that is long enough for you to keep your hand on one end, while your pup mouths on the other end. A rope toy works well. Keep your hand on one end of the toy while you present the other end to your pup.

Wiggle the toy in front of her to entice her to grab it and say "take it" just as her mouth closes around the toy (keeping ahold of the other end of the toy). Say "drop it" as you gently take the toy out of her mouth. Immediately give it back or throw it for her, so she learns you won't hoard it for yourself.

If your pup doesn't easily give up the toy, put a small piece of smelly food by her nose with your other hand (don't let go of the toy). As she spits out the toy to take the food, say "drop it," and immediately pop the food in her mouth as you praise her. Repeat just a few more times. "Drop it" should be a fun game. It's the flip side of "take it," it's *not* a punishment! Make it really fun for your dog.

Repeat the "take it" and "drop it" sequence several more times, then quit while she's still having fun. Repeat in short sessions throughout the day. Begin using various different objects and begin letting go of the toy as she "takes it." Once these two commands are well learned it will be easier to play fetch with her. It will also be easier to get items back that she has "stolen" from counters or from the kids' toy basket. by telling her to "drop it" and then *redirecting* her to a more appropriate item. Look for more details on stealing later in this chapter.

### Fetch

Fetch is an absolutely wonderful game for your dog. Once this game is learned, you can give your dog lots of exercise, play, and mental stimulation while you stand still!

There are many ways to teach this all-time favorite game. The first method we'll describe is for those dogs that show some interest in the ball (or other toy) and will pick it up in their mouths.

The first rule to this game (whatever method you use) is: *Never fetch for your dog, and never play chase games where you chase your dog around.* Chasing your dog will destroy any chance you have of getting him to come when called. Always be the one playing "hard to get".

Begin indoors at first, without other distractions. Use movement to attract your pup's attention by wiggling the ball in front of his face. As he orients toward the ball and gets excited about it, toss it 2 to 3 feet away. It's important not to toss it too far away at first.

Tossing it too far and losing the pup's attention is one of the most common mistakes people make in trying to teach fetch. Another big mistake is playing for too long, until the puppy loses interest and gets bored with the game.

As your puppy runs over to the ball, remain silent so as not to distract him. Just as his mouth closes around the ball (but not before that point) begin clapping, do a "play bow," and start running away from him. No need to say anything (you might distract him), just use your clapping and movement to attract your puppy toward you. As he gets to you with the ball in his mouth, tell him to "drop it" *as you take the ball.*

If he drops the ball on the way back to you, go ahead and throw it for him again (at least he started to bring it to you!). Gradually hold out for better and better retrieves before throwing the ball, using smooches and play bows to get him closer to you.

**The instant you get the ball from him, thow it!!** Don't stand there clutching it to your bosom telling him what a good dog he is and patting him on the head. He doesn't want patting or praise right now. Right now he wants the ball…*immediately!* So don't hoard the ball, *throw it!*

If he won't give up the ball, turn away from him as though you aren't interested in his silly ball, or walk away and end the game (he'll probably follow you and come closer when you stop). Or, try the next method.

An alternate method for teaching fetch is especially good for those dogs that have already learned how to play keep-away with the ball, and won't bring it back to you (at least not close enough for you to get it). *The first step is for you to stop chasing after your dog!* Who's suppose to be doing the fetching here anyway?

Start with two objects, preferably identical objects (such as two tennis balls). Begin as described previously: wiggle the ball in his face, toss it a couple feet away, as he picks it up clap, play bow, and run backwards. But this time bring the second, identical ball or toy out of your pocket and start waving it around, tossing it in the air and catching it yourself.

Your little ball thief will most likely become interested in the ball you have *because it's moving* and that makes it almost irresistible. He will probably drop the first ball at some point on his way over to you. That's fine, just say "drop it" as he spits it out, and keep teasing him with the second ball until he's almost to you. As he gets near, throw the second ball behind you so he comes racing up to you and past you to go get the second ball.

While he's busy getting the second ball, quietly go pick up the first one (thereby avoiding a game of keep-away) and start teasing him with the ball you just picked up. Repeat this sequence, but only do this 2 or 3 times in a row at most (for some dogs, once will be enough), then quit. *It's very important to stop the game while the puppy still wants more.* You can always play again later if he seems interested.

A third method for teaching fetch is for those dogs that won't put a toy or ball in their mouths, much less fetch it. They won't even follow the ball's movement with their eyes. For these dogs, use a toy that you can smear with food. Use some really wonderful food that your dog adores, like canned dog or cat food, liversausage, peanut butter, etc. As he licks the toy it will move a bit and he may begin to mouth it to get the food off. Put more food on and toss it just a foot or two in front of him. This time he should track the movement of the ball with his eyes because he knows it has food on it. He'll probably trot over to lick off the food.

When he (eventually) picks it up off the floor, cheer and clap and make a really big deal out of this important step he's taken. Gradually work up the distance you throw the toy, and gradually reduce the use of food on the toy. Many dogs can eventually be enticed to retrieve with this method.

## Catch

It's always fun to have a dog that catches things you throw. Begin (close to your puppy) by tossing food at your pup's nose. After a bit of trial and error, she'll begin to track it's path with her eyes, and then try to catch it. It takes practice to catch something-whether it's in your mouth or your hands, so don't laugh at her when the treat hits her in the face! Once she begins to catch most of the treats you toss from a short distance, you can begin to increase the distance and even put a word on it if you'd like. Say "catch" just as she opens her mouth to catch the treat. As she gets the hang of it you can start tossing soft toys to her.

## Frisbee

You may be anxious to teach your dog to play Frisbee, which can be a fun game for both of you, but it has it's drawbacks as well. Veterinarians see a lot of injuries associated with Frisbee playing. First of all it's essential to use a soft Frisbee made especially for dogs. Veterinarians see a lot of broken and cracked teeth from regular, hard Frisbees. They also see injuries from dogs jumping up and twisting to catch the Frisbee and then landing in all sorts of abnormal positions, putting undue strain on various parts of the body. This is a bad situation to put puppies in, so you shouldn't consider playing this game with your pup without first talking to your veterinarian.

## Find Mom or Dad

This is a great way to keep your puppy busy for awhile, both mentally and physically. And it's a fun game for the kids to play with the puppy. Begin with two people standing about 10-15 feet apart, facing each other. The first person (we'll call her "Mom") asks the pup, "Where's Dad?" At that instant Dad calls the pup while clapping and bending down to attract the puppy towards him.

When the pup gets there, Dad makes a big fuss over how brilliant she was, and gives her a treat, or plays with her. Then Dad asks, "Where's Mom?" and at that instant Mom calls the pup (just as Dad did). Mom gets very excited when the puppy gets to her, running away so the pup can chase her a little bit, or giving the puppy a belly rub, or whatever makes the puppy glad she came to Mom.

Repeat this sequence back and forth a few times, then be sure to quit while the puppy is still excited about the game. You don't want her to get bored with it. Next time you practice, begin to increase the distance between Mom and Dad. Work your way up to being in separate rooms (or behind separate trees outside).

As your pup begins to catch on to the game, just have one person send the puppy without the second person calling the pup anymore. Most pups catch on to this first part of the game pretty quickly. The second phase of this game is to help the puppy learn to distinguish various different people by name.

Up until now your pup doesn't really know Mom or Dad's name (though you may think that she does), she has only learned to run a pattern back and forth finding whichever person isn't present at the moment.

To help her learn to actually distinguish between various people, it helps to have 3 or 4 people for the pup to run between. Begin in a large circle (maybe 10-20 feet in diameter) and have Mom send the pup to Dad. If the pup goes to the wrong person, that person ignores the pup completely while Dad starts clapping and calling the pup. Dad praises and reinforces the pup for coming, then sends her to the next person. Again, if the puppy goes to the wrong person she gets ignored, and the target person calls to her. Through practice and repetition your pup can learn to distinguish between the names of each person in the group. Then you can start to teach her names of other people as well.

## Find the Toy

Teaching your pup to find a specific toy is a similar process to "Find Mom or Dad," except that the toy won't be able to call him! Start by teasing your pup just a bit with a favorite toy then "hide" it just by your side. Encourage him to find it; helping him if needs it. Then get really *excited* when he does find it. Let him play with it for a little while.

Next hide it behind your back. Then try hiding it somewhere close by. Gradually make the hiding places harder and further away. If your puppy is having any trouble finding the toy, run with him to the toy and help him find it.

Once this is going well you can begin to teach him the names of various toys by quietly taking away the wrong toy if he brings it to you, and encouraging him to try again to find the correct toy. Once he finds the correct toy make a really big deal over it and use it to play with him. Make him glad that he found it!

Now when he gets underfoot and tries to "help" you with a project, you can send him off on "a mission" to find some other member of the family, or a special toy. That will keep him busy for awhile, and he'll have lots of fun.

### Hide and Seek

Hide and seek is a wonderful game, especially useful for teaching your pup to come even when you are out of sight, and for rainy days, when the kids and/or dog are bored. See a description of how to play this game in chapter 2.

### Agility

Negotiating obstacles that require climbing, balancing, tunneling, walking on unfamiliar surfaces, and limited jumping can help develop your pup's coordination, balance, problem solving abilities, perseverance and confidence.

You don't need special agility equipment for your puppy to practice these skills. Find things to challenge your pup's ability in the course of your normal day. For example: your pup could climb over a small log during your walk in the woods, or crawl under the coffee table while you lure her with a toy. She could climb up and down stairs, go through a cardboard box you've opened on both ends, sit on a table, or "jump" through a hoola hoop you've suspended a few inches above the ground, and so on.

Just look around you and you're sure to find all sorts of opportunities to help your pup develop confidence (just keep safety in mind.) in herself and trust in you through agility exercises.

Be *cautious* about letting your pup do much jumping or twisting while she is young. If she does jump, keep the heights very low. Repeated jumping can be hard on her developing bones and joints. Check with your veterinarian if you have questions about what is safe for your puppy to do.

# WHEN PLAY BACKFIRES

Puppies learn an awful lot about the world through their play. If we want them to learn to be well mannered, we need to be sure that they are not getting the wrong messages from the games they play, and especially from the games we play with them.

## *Keep Away!!*

Dogs try desperately to get us to chase them. They love a good chase. But if we chase our pups around (at all) they quickly learn to play keep away. This includes playing keep away when we call them to come, or when they've "stolen" something they shouldn't have. Obviously we don't want that, especially if we're late for work and our puppy is heading off to Timbuktu.

**The rules to remember about this game are:**

1) **Never, ever chase after your puppy**, and don't let other members of your family do so either. You'll have to help children with this, they always want to chase the puppy.

2) **If you can't catch your pup or he won't come when you call, don't reinforce him by chasing after him.** Instead make yourself interesting: rattle the treat bag, toss a ball in the air, act like you are having a great time all by yourself, or roll in a cow pie to attract your pup's attention (boy, will he be jealous then!), just don't chase after your dog.

3) **If you must go get him (because it isn't safe not to), then follow quietly at a walk, don't run after him.**

## *Tug Of War*

This is a controversial subject. Some trainers feel you should never play tug of war with any dog. Some think it's a good game to play with most dogs. The decision of course is yours, but here are some things to consider:

Leaders control resources in a dog pack, so if you do play tug games, you should always "win" the prize. If your dog feels she "won" the prize and walks off with it, that sends her the wrong message about who is the leader of your pack (it should always be you and other humans, never your dog).

Tug of war also teaches your puppy to bite down as hard as she can, and put all of her body weight into pulling, biting and tugging an object, sometimes with growling included. It's easy for a pup to be confused about when this kind of behavior is appropriate. Your pup may try it with the new stockings you are putting on or with your child's shoelaces, etc.

On the other hand, dogs seem to love to play tug of war and some people can't seem to resist it either. So if you *are* going to play tug of war with your pup, at least *set some very clear rules*, and adhere to them diligently. The rules we would suggest (if you do decide to play tug of war with your dog) are:

- **Don't play tug of war if you have ever seen any signs of aggression from your pup.**

- **Don't let children play tug of war. Dogs can get carried away with kids because they often see children as having lower social status than themselves, so they can feel justified in doing whatever it takes to win the game.**

- **Don't let your kids watch you play tug of war with your dog or they may imitate it, and they'll always lose. Then you're in big trouble.**

- **Don't let your pup generalize to tugging on other items at other times, like leashes or clothing, etc.**

- **Play with only one toy. Keep this toy out of reach when not playing tug of war. You should be the only one that can initiate a game of tug or war. Never let your dog dictate when you'll play, for how long, or when you'll stop, that's *your* decision.**

- **If you can't get your dog to stop the game with a quiet "drop it" command, then don't play tug of war with your dog.**

- **Always, end up with the toy yourself. Don't let your dog walk away with it in the end. Leaders always win tug of war, and it's essential that you (and all humans) be the leader, not your dog. So take that wet slimy thing yourself, and put it up where your dog can't get it!**

## *Wrestling or Roughhousing*

Dogs settle a lot of social status or hierarchical issues during play with lots of subtle interactions that we don't even know about. So often they can walk away from a play session thinking they "won" when we didn't even realize there was a competition.

Another issue to think about with this kind of play is that we so easily condition our dogs that a hand moving toward them is to be snapped at, because that's what we taught them to do during play. Then we get upset with them when they playfully (but vigorously) snap at someone else's hand as that person goes to pet them. The dog gets a bad rap when he's only doing what we've taught him to do.

*Wrestling or roughhousing games encourage biting, jumping, growling, and pushiness* which only confuses the pup's understanding of how to behave around people.

Some training and behavioral problems can be traced back to the roughhousing type of play your pup gets. Does he persistently nip at your ankles as you try to heel with him? Does he jump up from behind and "tag" you with his teeth, because he's trying to get a game started? Are you having a hard time getting him to inhibit his bite and decrease his mouthing on people? *For these and many other behaviors, look to the kind of play your family does with your dog.* Often times there is some form of roughhousing or wrestling going on that is contributing to your pup's undesirable behaviors.

## *Stealing*

Dogs are natural born thieves! It's a trait that served their ancestors well, but we often find it to be inconvenient and annoying, as well as potentially dangerous to the pup.

First of all, *puppy proof the house to prevent problems,* and *supervise* the pup to pre-empt any attempts on her part to steal unauthorized items. If your pup has shown an interest in an item use booby traps, such as a pyramid of empty pop cans ready to topple down, or mousetraps for larger dogs, or something else that will startle the pup just as she goes to steal the item.

If she does get ahold of something she shouldn't have, resist the temptation to go chasing after your puppy. She'll only learn to play keep away and she will be that much harder to catch next time!

Ideally, you should teach your pup to "drop it" when you give a quiet command to do so. Until she learns that command well enough to do it while she's excited, *ignore her and her "prize" if possible.* She'll learn it's not such a great game after all, if no one will chase her or pay attention to her. Next time have a set-up ready so she gets corrected just as she tries to steal it.

When she has an item that you must get back right away, *use a distraction* to get her to drop it on her own. Go rattle the treat bag, or open the back door, or begin playing with a ball by yourself. Pretend that you don't even notice there is a dog around, but you just happen to be doing something terrific without her. Be fascinating; catch her attention in some way that entices her to come see what you're up to. If what you are doing is appealing enough, she will either drop her "prize" somewhere on her way over to you, or come over with the stolen item in her mouth. Once she comes over to get in on whatever game you are playing, ask her to "sit," "down," "sit" (or "stay" if she knows stay). If needed, you can put a piece of food near her nose to encourage her to drop her "prize," saying "drop it" as she opens her mouth to get the treat. But *don't give her the food right away, make her work for it.* Make her work first, so she doesn't think you are rewarding her stealing escapades.

Once she has *worked* for your attention, then you can reward her "sit" and "down" or divert her onto another activity while you quietly and unobtrusively repossess the stolen object. Then it's your job to prevent your pup from stealing it again through puppy proofing, and set-ups.

Remember, *prevention is an active training tool,* not just a way to avoid the problem. If you prevent your puppy from stealing tempting items, while at the same time teaching her which things she is allowed to play with, then stealing your belongings will not become part of her repertoire.

Exercise is an important part of prevention. Many dogs don't steal until they get bored and have excess energy to burn. They make up games to keep themselves busy and entertained; with stealing being a popular game. So exercise your puppy. Tire her out, and play with her often-you'll reduce problem behaviors if she gets enough exercise.

*Avoid situations where you reach in to grab things away from your puppy as she hides under a table or in a corner.* The last thing you want to do is teach her to be defensive about possessions and wary of hands reaching toward her. Instead, ignore her and do something distracting to catch her attention so she comes out on her own. Battling over possessions now can lead to more serious situations as your pup matures.

If your dog has ever been aggressive in situations like this, call right away to get a private session with an experienced behaviorist.

# Chapter 5

# RAISING CONFIDENT PUPPIES

**In this chapter:**

*Fear in puppies* ..........*47*
*Children & puppies* ......*49*
*Puppy Stay* ...............*50*
*Jumping up* ...............*51*
*Crate training* ............*52*

Very subtle signs of cautiousness in puppies can develop into full blown fears in adult dogs. Whether your pup shows subtle or obvious signs of fear, it's best to help him deal with his worries now, while he's a youngster. Let's look at some examples of common fears and how they might be made better or worse depending on how they are handled.

When Cassidy went for his first visit to the vet he got poked, jabbed, prodded and held down forcibly while they clipped his nails, wormed him, gave him his vaccinations, and checked him over. He whined, yelped and squirmed a lot and was wide eyed and frightened much of the time. His new owner tried to make him feel better by petting him while he whined and soothing him with lots of: "it's okay Cassidy, it's all right, don't be afraid…" in her most comforting voice, but it didn't seem to help.

This experience will probably make Cassidy wary of the vet's office next time he has to go there. He may get worse with each visit until he becomes an adult dog that is very difficult to handle at the vet's office. How could this have been handled differently to help Cassidy become more comfortable with his trips to the vet?

*First impressions are powerful,* so making that first visit as stress free and fun as possible would have a lasting effect on Cassidy.

First of all his owners could have tried to schedule an appointment when the vet wasn't busy, so the staff could take a few extra minutes with Cassidy. They could have greeted him, petted him and given him a few treats while he got a chance to relax in the new surroundings. It also would have helped him if his new owner praised him when he acted confident.

It would also have been a good idea to schedule only the absolute necessities on the first visit to the vet, making it as pain free and pleasant as possible. Giving Cassidy treats while he was just getting his shots, would have helped him focus on the food more, and the fear less. His owners could have also brought a toy and played with Cassidy before, and after the actual exam. Definitely skip the nail trim on the first visit!

Cassidy may have enjoyed the attention, treats and play enough that he would be relaxed and happy next time he went back to visit his veterinarian.

Jake is another puppy with a different problem. Every once in while his owners open the closet at the end of the hall, the one where the monster lives, and they let it out to terrorize poor Jake. Although the family thinks it's pretty cute the way Jake viciously attacks the noisy creature (they call it a "vacuum") and then jumps back to a safe distance, Jake is very serious. They think it's even funnier when they point the monster right at him and have it chase him! He runs to hide in the other room while they have a good laugh about it.

One day they decide Jake is getting too old for this so they take him by the collar and drag him to the noisy, smelly monster. Jake is so frightened he snaps at the monster and then at his owner's hands in a panicked attempt to get away to safety. His owner's decide to give up and they start putting Jake in the yard whenever they vacuum.

Jake learned several things here that his owners did not intend to teach him. One of the things Jake learned was that snapping at things he's frightened of works (including people who "trap" him in fearful situations). He'll probably try that strategy again sometime, much to his owner's dismay.

Jake could be helped to overcome his fear by pairing something he loves with what scares him. In this case Jake's favorite game is fetch, and what scares him is the vacuum.

Jake's family could help him feel really good (by playing fetch) *before* the vacuum is ever brought out. They can then begin to play fetch with Jake while the vacuum just sits quietly (turned off) in the next room.

Next they can play fetch with Jake, and during the game turn the vacuum on for *just a second,* then off again immediately.

As Jake comes to accept these brief moments of noise in the middle of his wonderful playtime, the vacuum can be turned on for slightly longer periods while they continue to play fetch with him. Step by step the family could increase the duration of the time the vacuum is on and move it slightly closer to where Jake is playing.

Eventually, Jake will be able to be in the same room with the vacuum running and not be bothered by it.

This process needs to be done at whatever pace Jake's comfort level dictates. If he gets too nervous to play (or take a treat) then they need to back off again and build up more slowly. It may take a few days, or many weeks. Jake's family can help him learn to overcome any other such fears one by one, so Jake learns to be more confident about new things.

## CHILDREN AND PUPPIES

Following is a checklist of things to remember when children and dogs mix:

- Children and puppies should not be together unsupervised. Period.

- Children don't know what hurts or scares puppies. So *if you don't protect your puppy from children, you'll be forcing your puppy to protect himself.*

- Puppies will tolerate a tremendous amount that they later will not tolerate as adults. So don't let the fact that your 5 month old puppy tolerates certain types of behavior from children now lull you into thinking that he always will.

- Involve children in the training of your pup as soon as they are able, but *you've got to monitor them.* Children tend to go to extremes with their commands, almost universally. Kids repeat commands endlessly and don't follow through, so your pup learns to ignore commands.

- Teach children the right way to approach and pet your puppy. In general they should be kind and gentle to the puppy and it's up to you to show them how. Teach them to pet the pup on his chest and cheeks rather than slapping him on the top of his head.

- Avoid picking up puppies whenever possible. (For one thing, they need to learn how to walk with you from place to place rather than being airlifted the rest of their lives! Adults with small dogs, this means you too.) Don't let kids carry your puppy around either. Puppies can develop a real aversion to this (being grabbed, squeezed, smushed, and carried), and it may elicit defensive aggression from them as they mature.

- *Don't let your puppy play chase games with children* where the puppy chases the kids (or the kids chase the puppy). Running, giggling, screaming kids are just too much for most puppies, causing the pup to become inappropriate with the kids. Instead put the pup in another room or his crate for a little while, or leash him to you. (*Supervised* "come" games where the child stops as the

49

puppy approaches are fine as long as the pup isn't using his mouth when he gets to the child.)

- Teach children to play appropriately with your pup (see chapter 4 on Play). Hide and seek, catch, fetch, find Mom or Dad or a particular toy, or agility exercises can all be good games for children to play with puppies. Limit the amount of time the kids and pup are allowed to frolic together, they can both get carried away if left together for long periods. It also helps to have the pup burn off a little energy before playing with children.

- Keep in mind that if a pup spends an excessive amount of time running around and barking in the house now, he will be rowdy in the house as an adult! Don't encourage rowdy behavior in the house from your pup anymore than you would encourage your children to play softball in the dining room near the family's heirloom china!

- You can help your children each teach the puppy a different trick. But again, supervise the training as well as the use of the trick (no dog wants to rollover 57 times in one day!).

- Although dogs need times to be left alone, and kids must be taught that sometimes one should "let sleeping dogs lie," avoid setting up a place in your house where no one dare bother the dog or you may end up with problems later.

- It's critically important to *teach children never to approach strange dogs* without permission from you *and* the dog's owner. Not all dogs will be as friendly as your pup. And even friendly dogs may get frightened by children running up unannounced and hugging them.

## PUPPY STAY

Our version of a "stay" for young pups is really more of a pause than a stay! Try to keep it so short that your pup can't possibly get it wrong. That may mean half a second at first. Progress very slowly using lots of patience.

Begin by asking your pup to "sit." With your hand flat, palm facing outward toward your pup (but near your body-don't wave your fingers in your pup's face), say "stay" in a flat or slowly descending tone. Then freeze. Don't move, don't breathe! After a heartbeat or two, release your pup from stay by saying "free" or "okay" while play bowing and dancing backwards, clapping your hands on your legs, and rewarding the pup with a treat. (You want the pup to hear a clear acoustic signal that means they are released, and also get a clear visual signal as well.)

There you have it: a puppy stay! Spend about a week doing these ultra short stays, 2 or 3 at a time, scattered throughout your day, and in lots of different locations.

Gradually build up the amount of time the pup will hold still. It may take weeks to build up to 30 seconds in a quiet room with no distractions. That's fine, go at your puppy's pace. As your pup ages, and develops a more solid stay, start returning to her and giving her a treat while she's still staying. Make staying even more fun than the release.

Don't try to work on long stays (over a minute) now, your pup is too young for that. Once your pup can "stay" for 30 seconds to a minute, begin to add in minor distractions, but only expect a half second "stay," just as when you started. Work up your time again, with *distractions*. Lastly, begin to take one step backwards (starting with half second stays again if needed) at a time. Increase the distance between you and your pup very slowly.

The biggest mistake people make in teaching stay is trying to jump from step 1 to 100. Your pup needs those other steps in between, just as you did when you learned a new skill that required concentration. It can take 2 years to get a solid off leash "stay," in the face of major distractions. Asking your pup to sit-stay at the front door when guests arrive is like astrophysics to your puppy!

## JUMPING UP

Puppies begin jumping on people when they are very, very young. They are trying to get near our faces and get our attention in order to greet us. We think it's sweet and cute when they are little. We bend over and pet them, scratch them, talk to them or even pick them up. In other words, we *reinforce them for jumping up on us.*

Then they grow taller, get heavier, grow bigger nails, and become more boisterous in their jumping up, and now it's not so cute. But our pups are jumping on us now partially because we inadvertently taught them to.

How do we reverse that unintentional training? We do it by becoming more aware of what we are or are not reinforcing during greetings, or other times that they jump on us. If we begin to reinforce the "four paws on the floor" policy, we will begin to see their feet on the floor more often!

It's easy to teach your dog to be hysterical and out of control when greeting you (and other people) by making a habit of excited, energetic greetings. So instead, when you first come home, greet your pup with a quiet, low key "hello" and a light touch under the chin or on the side of the face and leave it at that. Save more vigorous or excitable interactions for 10–15 minutes after you get home, but make that initial greeting rather uneventful. When you do greet him *only give him the attention he wants when he has 4 feet on the floor!*

If he jumps on you use *your body* to block him *on his way up*, before the paws even make contact.

**Don't push him down with your hands,** this seems to just stimulate more jumping. Simply move into him with your hip or leg (don't try to jab him with your knee), taking control of the space in front of him, and imposing your height over him. Immediately ask for a "sit." The instant he complies, squat down to his level and give him the attention he wants (or an occasional treat with attention). If he's back up as soon as you start to squat down, block him with your body again, and try petting him quietly on his chest (not on the top of his head).

Or…try folding your arms in and immediately turning 180° away from him *just as he begins to jump up.* If he plants four paws on the floor looking up at you, then whip around, and quickly squat down to greet him. Reinforce the fact that he has four feet on the floor! Teach your kids, your friends, and your neighbors to do this also.

The success of both of these methods depends on your timing. If you respond *before* he touches you with his paws, he will quickly learn that it gets him nowhere to attempt to jump on you.

Also note that both of these methods instruct your pup about what "right" is, and that both methods avoid hurting or scaring him. Don't knee him in the chest, step on his toes, kick at him, or any other method that you may have heard about that can hurt or frighten him.

## CRATE TRAINING

If puppies are confined in some way whenever you can't supervise them, they will be prevented from learning a lot of bad habits or getting themselves hurt. Remember that prevention of bad habits is a powerful training tool. Therefore, it only makes sense to confine your pup in some way when you aren't with her. Use confinement when:

- You are too busy to watch your pup.

- You are leaving the house for awhile.

- Your puppy is being wild and crazy and needs a little "time out".

- When you are sleeping.

Confinement can be in a dog crate or kennel like the plastic airline type or a wire crate. With a wire crate it is a good idea to cover the top and 3 sides of it so your pup feels enclosed. Confinement can also be in a small puppy proofed room, such as a vinyl floored laundry room, kitchen, or bathroom. Put a gate across the doorway if you can, rather than shutting the door.

If you are using a crate, put it off to one side, or in a corner, so it is a little bit out of the way of traffic, in a room that you use quite a bit. Don't exile your pup to some lonely spot in the house. On the other hand, don't put it out in the middle of a busy room. Ideally the crate is in your bedroom so your puppy isn't alone at night.

## *Teaching your Pup to Enjoy the Crate*

If your pup is not accustomed to being left in a crate or room take it slowly, one step at a time to start out. Begin with your pup near the crate, off leash (don't force any part of this, instead entice) with the crate door open. Show him that you have a really wonderful treat (put the treat 1/4 of an inch from his nose). Move the treat slowly toward the crate door, "luring" him toward the crate with the food.

Toss the treat just inside the crate. Hopefully he will reach his head into the crate opening to get the treat. It doesn't matter that he doesn't go all the way in at first, you can build up to that by throwing the treat farther into his crate each time you practice this. (If food doesn't tempt him, try using a favorite toy and lots of quiet praise.)

*Leave the door open for now.* Put a command on entering the crate by telling your pup "kennel" or "go to bed" *as he enters* the kennel to get the treat. If he is too afraid to go in at all, then set the treat on the floor just outside the kennel door and let him take his time. Get him comfortable eating it *outside*, but near the crate, before trying to put the food *just inside* the door. Make sure he's comfortable at each stage before moving the food farther and farther into the crate. Repeat this game 4–6 times each session. Keep it fun, don't force or drag him into the crate, this could easily make him more afraid of his crate.

Repeat this game several times a day for a few more days, then begin shutting the door for *just a second* while he is in there eating his treats. Work up to several seconds with the door shut. You can put a hollow toy (stuffed with treats) in the kennel with him. As he busily works on getting the treats out of the toy, close the kennel door for longer and longer periods of time. He'll probably be so busy with the toy he won't notice or mind that the door is closed. Feeding him his meals in the kennel also helps him learn to be comfortable in there.

You are progressively teaching him, step by step, that wonderful things happen while he's in his kennel. You may even find him wandering into the kennel for a nap now and then. Most pups learn to enjoy their own special place, whether it is a kennel or their bed in a small room.

As you lengthen the time that he is shut in his crate with the door closed, at some point he is bound to try barking or whining to get out. This is natural, it's his way of trying to let you know he wants your company. It is important however that you *do not* inadvertently reinforce the barking or whining by letting him out (or telling him "it's okay") *while* he's making a fuss. Instead, ignore him until he quiets down on his own. If not reinforced for making a fuss, most pups will learn to settle down and be quiet when left in their kennel or room.

If you need to get him out of the kennel while he's crying or barking, distract him with a noise (click of the tongue, tap on the wall, anything that gets his attention) to get him quiet for a moment. The *instant* that he is quiet you can let him out of the kennel.

*Try to avoid shouting at him.* You are basically barking back at him! For many dogs this just reinforces their vocal efforts, even though you probably view it as negative attention. To your dog it's attention none the less. It is rarely effective for stopping barking or whining, especially in the long run.

*Tire him out before putting him in the crate.* Give him something safe to chew on (like a Nylabone, or a Kong™), and be sure he's been outside before he goes in his crate. He will most likely sleep if all his needs are tended to before you put him in the crate. And don't leave him in there for endless hours. Especially with a young pup, limit the time he's left alone to just a few hours at a time. Crates *can* be overused. But if used judiciously they can be one of your best allies in teaching your pup how to be calm and quiet in the house.

### Crates For Traveling

Crates are also great for traveling with your dog. If you plan to travel with him at all, it will be to your advantage and his to have him crate trained before you take a trip. Start while he is young so the crate becomes a familiar and comfortable place for him before you hit the road. A crate is also a safe place for dogs to be when they are in the car.

# Chapter 6

# ADOLESCENCE & OTHER QUANDARIES

**In this chapter:**

Ignoring commands. .......55
Dog to dog interactions ..56
Submissive urination .....57
Multiple dog households .58
Puppies home alone ......59
Car sickness................60
Exercise.....................60
Barking.....................61
What's next?..............63

**M**y pup used to be so good. Now he sometimes seems to be ignoring me. What's going on?

Adolescence is a time of change for your pup just as it is for human teenagers. Hormones run amuck, pups begin to get more independent, and they begin testing their limits (and your patience!). Your previously sweet pup may be impossible one day and back to sweet the next. Somewhere between 4 1/2 months to 6 months of age is when you usually see the crash. Then it's pretty up and down for the next several months. Around a year and a half to 2 years they tend to be sweet again. But your dog isn't fully mature and grown up until about 2 1/2 to 3 years of age.

What should you do when your adolescent becomes willful? Just calmly and quietly carry through. Don't over react, instead just get your pup to do as you have asked. No need to shout or use strong physical corrections, just be persistent. Repeat visual signals, use body blocks and (if need be) physically place him; quickly but gently. Try to avoid the "hands on approach" if possible, but in any case, see to it that the command is followed. Don't worry if it takes some time to get it done, as long as it *does* get done in the end.

**Carry through on commands you've given.** Don't give up and walk away (or let your pup walk away!) or your pup will learn that he can ignore you, which will quickly become a habit!

**Only give commands when you intend to carry through, and are able to do so.** For example: don't let him off leash at the park with a gang of puppy hooligans when *you know* he ran off the last two times you let him loose to play there. You *know* it will happen again, so don't give him the chance to get it wrong again! Instead have him drag a long line so if he starts to run away with his friends after you've called him to "come," you'll have some way to prevent him from totally ignoring you. *Use the leash to stop him* if needed, and *then use motivation* to get him to come (don't reel him in, the purpose of the leash is that of a safety net, not a fishing line).

**Make your pup work for a living.** Put a price on everything he wants. For example: have him "sit" and do a brief "stay" for his dinner; call him to "come" across the room to you, away from the door when he wants to go outside to play; have him "down" before you throw his tennis ball; and so on.

**Vary the jobs and rewards** so he never knows what he'll be asked to do next. Besides keeping your adolescent busy, you'll be reminding him to pay attention!

**Exercise, exercise, exercise!** Give your pup as much exercise as your vet will allow. Tired pups are less bored and get into less trouble.

Pups usually have a couple of periods in their lives when they become more easily frightened by things. These times are often referred to as "fear periods." There seems to be one during early adolescence-at around 6 to 9 months. Be aware that it might happen to your pup, and be ready to help him through it (see chapter 5).

## WHY WOULD A DOG THAT HAS ALWAYS PLAYED NICELY WITH MY PUP SUDDENLY SNAP AND GROWL AT HER?

### *Because your pup is growing up!*

- In effect, her "puppy license" has expired. Although you may not see much noticeable change in her attitude and behavior toward other dogs, they do! They've noticed that she has grown up, and while they may have allowed her to jump on their heads (and lots of other puppy behaviors) while she was a baby, they are now giving fair warning that those sort of puppy shenanigans are no longer acceptable.

- In human terms it might be like a 5 year old girl walking up to a police officer and trying to take his gun-he would act much differently if a young child did this than if an 18 year old boy (or girl) tried to do the same! In your pup's case, the other dogs are simply saying "it's time to act like an adult, and live by adult rules."

- If your puppy is an unneutered male you may notice even stronger reactions from other dogs (and from your pup). The testosterone levels in an adolescent male dog are more than *ten times* higher than they will be when he's an adult. This has a big impact on how other dogs react to your adolescent male, as well as affecting his behavior towards others.

- If another dog snaps at your pup, it may look frightening, but dogs do occasionally communicate to other dogs by displaying their teeth. Think about it, they can't very well send their lawyers in to settle things for them, now can they?

- Reactions to your pup will vary from one dog to another; much as one person might react differently to you than another would. If you accidentally stepped on someone's toes while waiting in line, the other person might: ignore it, give you a glance and an understanding smile, shoot you a glare of disapproval, or they might turn around and say: "#*#@#%*!" and step on your toes. Dogs have equally variable responses. What is *not* normal is a dog who does not inhibit itself. If your pup or the other dog doesn't stop when one of them gives in, then intervene to keep things from escalating.

- To avoid tension when meeting unfamiliar dogs try to keep the leashes loose; don't stare at the dogs; don't convey any of your nervousness to your dog (through the leash tension, your voice, or movements). Act at ease and confident so your pup doesn't get worried about the approaching dog. Lessen any tension on greeting by defusing the situation and redirecting your pup. For example you could say in a cheerful voice "OK, lets go for a walk!"

- If your pup does get scared by another dog, don't make a fuss! Try to act calm and matter-of-fact, so she will feel confident and safe because of the certainty you show her. Try to meet other friendly dogs that look like the one that scared her. So, if a black Lab frightened her, find some friendly black Labs for her to play with, so she doesn't learn to fear all big black dogs that she meets.

- An occasional spat is a normal part of being an adolescent pup, but if it happens often or is ever severe, contact a professional for help in figuring out why, and to get advice on how to handle these situations.

## MY PUPPY URINATES WHEN I GREET HIM. WHY? AND WHAT CAN I DO ABOUT IT?

This is called *submissive urination*. Most pups will outgrow it, but there are things you can do to help assure that and to speed it along. Here are some tips:

- Never scold your pup for doing this, it will just make the problem worse. He's trying his best to tell you how submissive he is. Scolding will just make him try harder, and your shoes will get wetter. Try to greet him on a vinyl floor or outside, so it isn't a problem to clean it up.

- Keep your good-byes and homecomings low key. Let your pup think that having you come and go is no big deal.

- Don't lean over your pup as you great him. Instead kneel down, with your weight leaning slightly back away from him.

- Get in the habit of coming in the door flinging food off to one side or the other, while you walk straight ahead, ignoring the puppy. This seems to help switch the pup out of greeting mode and into eating mode.

- Be careful about yelling at your pup, in general, at any time, or being harsh with him. A pup that urinates submissively needs a lot of confidence building with you and with life in general.

- Teach your guests to follow these guidelines too.

## ARE THERE ANY SPECIAL CONSIDERATIONS WITH MULTIPLE-DOG HOUSEHOLDS?

### *Yes, a few...*

- It's usually fine to let your puppy play with any older dogs in the house if they seem to be getting along well. Dogs play by using their teeth, biting, snarling, growling, barking...basically being dogs! Don't be too concerned about the noises they make or the teeth you see unless one of them seems frightened, or one gets carried away and seems excessive. If so, then step in and break it up.

- Don't let them play uninterrupted for hours on end. You want your puppy to learn that you are also a great source of fun. If your pup spends *all* of her time with your other dog(s), then you become the "odd man out," the old "wet blanket" who just doesn't compare. So set a balance in your puppy's playtime.

- It's usually a good idea to supervise the play as well, so when you leave the house they should probably be kept separated by a gate or kennel until the puppy is a little older.

- If an old, or very submissive dog is being harassed by the puppy, stop the pup. Your older dog deserves some peace and quiet!

- If your adult dog(s) *never* corrects the pup for rude behavior, and puts up with all kinds of abuse from the puppy, then you may need to step in and pull the puppy off occasionally, so she doesn't learn to be a bully. Be sure your pup *does* play with dogs who set limits!

- Spend some time working separately with each dog. You want each of them to bond with you, to get individualized attention and guidance in training, and to learn that *you* are the key to all good things in life.

- Don't try to set up one dog or another as "alpha" over the other(s). You should be the clear leader, on the top rung, with any and all dogs in the house being loved, cherished, and *at the bottom* of the social hierarchy ladder!

## WHAT CAN I DO TO HELP MY PUPPY MANAGE WHEN I HAVE TO LEAVE HIM ALONE?

- Give your pup plenty of exercise before leaving him alone. For very quiet pups at least half an hour twice a day of energetic play is needed. Double or triple that amount for an active, high energy pup!

- Confine your pup to a safe area before you leave. This could be a crate or a small room that has been puppy proofed and has vinyl or tile floors.

- Make sure he's "gone" outside (with supervision and a treat) before confining him.

- Provide him with *safe* toys while in his crate. Rotate toys from day to day to keep his interest. *Many toys and chews are not safe* to leave with an unattended dog. Do got give rawhide to an unattended pup. Some veterinarians advise against rawhide at any time, others recommend it. Discuss it with your veterinarian. Only allow your pup access to toys like rope bones, squeaky toys, or stuffed animals when you are there to supervise. They can all be very dangerous if chewed into smaller pieces.

- Safe toys that you can leave with him in his crate include Kong™ toys and goodie space ships with peanut butter or other food stuffed inside. Trying to get the food out of these toys can keep a pup occupied for 15 minutes to an hour or more, depending on the puppy. Nylabones are another safe choice.

- **Make your exits and entrances low key.** Your pup can easily learn to be hysterical to everyone who comes through your door if he gets elaborate, emotional greetings on a routine basis. Instead, give just a quiet hello, and then mostly ignore your pup until you've been home for 10-20 minutes. You can save the excitement for later in the day, but *keep it low key when you first get home.* Don't fawn over your pup as you leave either, instead act as though it's no big deal. This can help prevent anxiety in your puppy while you are gone.

- Leaving a radio playing on a quiet classical or "easy listening" station (avoid hard rock and talk radio stations) while you are gone. This can help to mask outside noises and might make your pup feel less alone.

- After you've provided him with a chance to go outside, and with exercise, toys, and a comfortable, safe place, go ahead and leave him for a few hours without worry. He'll probably sleep while you are gone.

## MY PUPPY GETS CAR SICK. WILL SHE EVER BE ABLE TO RIDE IN THE CAR WITHOUT GETTING SICK?

### Yes, she certainly will!

Most puppies outgrow car sickness as they grow up. In young puppies the inner ear canal is not completely developed, which can cause nausea and vomiting with the motion of a moving car. Nervousness or fear of the car may magnify this effect.

Help her to overcome her fears by associating wonderful things with the car and car rides. Try playing with her in the car, with a toy, while the doors are open (engine off, car in the driveway). Give her meals to her in the car. Or have someone ride with her during very short daily trips, feeding her little bits of liver. Just go a block at first, then get out and take her on a fun little walk. Drive her a little further each time.

If she's very afraid of the car, start with feeding the liver just outside of the car while it is motionless in the driveway with the engine off. Then feed her just inside the car door, then further inside the car, then all the way inside with the engine running but no movement, then with movement, but only in and out of the driveway, and so on. Build up *gradually,* making her comfortable at each level before progressing to the next.

Before long trips it's usually best not to feed your pup for several hours before leaving. Work on the "liver therapy" at a separate time, using toys instead of food to jolly her up on longer trips.

Covered crates inside the car can also be very helpful. Your pup will move around less, and may feel less dizzied by the world rushing by; which can reduce her chances of getting sick in the car. A crate is also a good safety measure for her, and for the driver whom she might distract.

## DO DOGS REALLY NEED MUCH EXERCISE?

### Yes Absolutely!

Dogs need a lot of running, preferably off leash (in a safe area). A walk around the block once or twice a day is not enough exercise for most dogs, unless it's a very young pup, or there are extenuating circumstances. Many behavioral problems can be traced back to boredom and inactivity in family dogs, so prevent problems by giving your dog plenty of exercise, play, and training.

Playing fetch is great exercise that doesn't involve much effort on your part. Once your pup is retrieving well (see "Fetch" in chapter 4), try a tennis racket, or one of the special ball launchers made to help you throw the ball farther while saving your arm (you can find them in pet stores or dog supply catalogs). Walks in the woods or fields are good exercise. Another great way to exercise your pup is to let him play with another dog; they're pretty efficient at wearing one another out!

Biking or jogging with you can be a good form of exercise for adult dogs, but can cause problems in puppies whose bones and joints aren't finished developing. The age that it is safe to start them out on this sort of exercise varies by breed: it can be anywhere from 1 year to 18 months or even later. Be sure to check with your veterinarian before doing either of these forms of exercise with your pup. Regardless of your dog's age, avoid frequent running on hard pavement which is hard on any dog.

## HELP! MY PUPPY JUST STARTED BARKING A LOT. WILL SHE OUTGROW IT?

*Not necessarily.*
Excessive barking as a pup can lead to excessive barking as an adult.

**Begin by looking at why your pup is barking.** Dogs bark for a number of reasons, some common ones include: excitement, seeking attention, loneliness, anxiety, or boredom. If you remove the cause, you can reduce your pup's tendency to bark, and *now* is the time to do it.

For example: if your pup barks when other dogs are playing, she might be both excited and a little bit nervous or scared to join in. Try distracting her each time she barks and see if you can get the other dogs to greet her quietly and give her a chance to join in on something more sedate, building her courage up to the livelier level of play.

If your pup barks at you to get attention, or to demand that you give her something, then be careful *not* to reinforce that behavior. *Ignore her completely until she is quiet,* turn your head away or turn your back on her if she is being very pushy. You could even leave the room until she quiets down. As soon as she is quiet, ask her to do something for you (sit, down, etc.) then give her the attention she wants. If she is demanding play, redirect her by giving some commands (sit, down, etc.), then playing with her once she is quiet. Be careful not to let her train you to respond to *her* demands!

Dogs left outside for long periods, especially those that are chained out, often develop a bad barking habit. Perhaps it begins out of nervousness, loneliness, boredom, or a feeling that you left her out there "on guard duty." Many dogs become stressed by this "responsibility" and overreact by barking at every little thing. This can lead to a lot of territorial behaviors that can become problematic as she matures. It can also confuse her about her status in her human "pack." Training her how to be good in the house, then keeping her inside when you are gone, and allowing her to spend more time with you while you are home, will avoid this type of barking problem.

Sometimes we inadvertently teach our pups to bark by reinforcing barking, without realizing it. If your pup barks at a stranger at your door, and you encourage her because you think she is being "brave" or "cute," you'll soon have a dog that barks excessively at people who come to your house. You'll probably have a hard time getting her to stop when you want her to. She may continue to develop more aggressive responses to people at your door, as she gets older.

Or do you soothe her, pet her, and tell her "it's okay" while trying to calm her? She might conclude that you *like it* when she barks at the door (petting and soothing voices saying "okay" are reinforcements). She will probably become more vigorous with her barking each time someone comes over to your house.

**Instead of giving her either of these inadvertent messages, interrupt her barking.** Then introduce her to the person in a confident, friendly manner so she knows it's okay for that person to be there. Have the other person give her some treats (tossing them to her if she's afraid to get close), and help her learn that people are friendly!

**Don't ever encourage your dog to bark at people.** Most likely her instinct to protect your territory will develop on it's own when she is 2 to 3 years old. She'll "alert bark" if there is something odd going on, even though you haven't encouraged barking. *Teaching your dog to be suspicious of people will not develop a good watchdog-it will develop a time bomb!* If you develop a good relationship with her, socialize her extensively, and train her in basic manners, she will be much more likely to become a good watchdog than if you encourage her to be aggressive or cautious towards people. Also, be cautious about correcting her if she is at all fearful of unfamiliar people. In this case, have visitors throw treats to her when they arrive, so she learns to love having company!

To get some control over your pup's barking regardless of the reason she is barking, teach her a command that means "that first bark or two was fine, but now I want you to be quiet." Use a one word command like "Enough!" You can teach "Enough!" by *presenting a stimulus that elicits barking* (like making a noise that causes her to bark), *then taking it away* (stop knocking or whatever) when you say "Enough." This way you can control when she barks and when she stops.

Begin when she is not in a barky mood so that you can get her to stop more easily. Elicit barking, then make a small noise (tongue click or finger snap, etc.) to interrupt her barking and draw her attention to you and say "enough". If she stops barking, give her a treat, then praise her. If she is more persistent in her barking, you can put a smelly treat *right* by her nose to catch her attention and interrupt her barking. *Be sure to say "Enough" just before she quiets.* Don't give her the food yet, wait for a few seconds, then give her the treat and praise her. Gradually extend the time she is quiet before she gets the treat. Once she stops barking, redirect her to some other activity. Your goal is to have her:

1) Hear the word "Enough" just before she stops barking (later you can say "enough" *while* she's barking to get her to stop).

2) Get the treat and praise only when she's quiet.

3) Wait long enough between the barking and the treat that she does not think the treat was *for* barking! It's important that she comes to understand the treat was for silence.

Practice in short, frequent sessions.


## WHAT'S NEXT?

### *Keep working with your puppy!!*
You're well on your way to a polite, well mannered family dog, but this is just the start. Your puppy needs continuing socialization, and proofing through distractions on the basic commands covered in this book. There are also other new commands that he should learn as part of his education in family manners, so keep attending classes or getting training help. *Continue to train your pup!* You wouldn't pull your child out of school in 3rd grade, would you?

Keep getting him out and about so he continues to be exposed to other people and other dogs. Enroll in fun, positive training classes, and stick with them until your dog will *always* listen to you when he's off leash.

Read more books, watch some videos, or go to some seminars. The more you learn about how your dog *thinks, learns* and *communicates,* the more joyful your relationship will be. Remember that involving her in family activities and allowing her more freedom (and you less worry) comes from training: it comes from actively raising her to be the dog you want.

Congratulations on a journey well started, and best wishes for a long and happy life together.